PRACTICAL
SUPERVISION
FOR
COUNSELLORS
WHO WORK
WITH YOUNG
PEOPLE

by the same author

Working with Anger and Young People
ISBN 978 1 84310 466 7
eISBN 978 1 84642 538 7

Feeling Like Crap
Young People and the Meaning of Self-Esteem
ISBN 978 1 84310 682 1
eISBN 978 1 84642 819 7

Listening to Young People in School, Youth Work and Counselling
ISBN 978 1 85302 909 7
eISBN 978 1 84642 201 0

Essential Listening Skills for Busy School Staff
What to Say When You Don't Know What to Say
ISBN 978 1 84905 565 9
eISBN 978 1 78450 000 9

School Counsellors Working with Young People and Staff
A Whole-School Approach
ISBN 978 1 84905 460 7
eISBN 978 0 85700 838 1

Young People in Love and in Hate
ISBN 978 1 84905 055 5
eISBN 978 0 85700 202 0

Horny and Hormonal
Young People, Sex and the Anxieties of Sexuality
ISBN 978 1 78592 031 8
eISBN 978 1 78450 278 2

Young People and the Curse of Ordinariness
ISBN 978 1 84905 185 9
eISBN 978 0 85700 407 9

Young People, Death and the Unfairness of Everything
ISBN 978 1 84905 320 4
eISBN 978 0 85700 662 2

PRACTICAL SUPERVISION
FOR
COUNSELLORS WHO WORK WITH YOUNG PEOPLE

Nick Luxmoore

Jessica Kingsley *Publishers*
London and Philadelphia

First published in 2017
by Jessica Kingsley Publishers
73 Collier Street
London N1 9BE, UK
and
400 Market Street, Suite 400
Philadelphia, PA 19106, USA

www.jkp.com

Copyright © Nick Luxmoore 2017

Front cover image source: Shutterstock®.

Library of Congress Cataloging in Publication Data
A CIP catalog record for this book is available from the Library of Congress

British Library Cataloguing in Publication Data
A CIP catalogue record for this book is available from the British Library

ISBN 978 1 78592 285 5
eISBN 978 1 78450 589 9

Printed and bound in Great Britain

For Sue Douglas

Acknowledgements

A version of Chapter 4 was published by BACP as 'Containing the angry client' in June 2016 *BACP Children and Young People* journal.

A version of Chapter 6 was published by BACP as 'On not being weird' in June 2015 *BACP Children and Young People* journal.

A version of Chapter 12 was published by BACP as 'Anger management: The myth' in September 2011 *BACP Children and Young People* journal.

A version of Chapter 22 was published by BACP as 'What's the point of fathers?' in December 2016 *BACP Children and Young People* journal.

A version of Chapter 23 was published by BACP as 'Just to say that I've failed… again!' in December 2015 *BACP Children and Young People* journal.

I'm grateful to Kathy Peto, Debbie Lee, Professor Chris Mowles and Jane Campbell for reading and commenting on earlier drafts of this book. Thanks also to my past and present supervisees, to my first supervisor, Sue Douglas, and to my current supervisor, Jane Campbell. Big thanks to Sarah Knight who organizes the training. And special thanks and love to the three people who supervise me most rigorously: Kathy, Frances and Julia.

Contents

1

Introduction

This isn't a book of supervision theory, nor is it a book about how to be a supervisor. Rather, it's a book about what goes on in supervision sessions with counsellors who work with young people. What gets talked about? Which issues recur with young people and how are they addressed in supervision? What helps counsellors to move on when they're stuck? The book doesn't aim to cover every issue that counsellors working with young people will ever want to talk about in supervision – a book like that would run to several volumes – but it does explore the issues that preoccupy most counsellors most of the time.

In many walks of life, being 'supervised' means being told what to do by a superior, whereas in counselling supervision, the counsellor arrives hoping to learn, to test hypotheses, to keep tabs on his or her own unconscious processes so that they don't interfere unhelpfully with the work. The supervisor listens and tries to make sense of whatever the counsellor is bringing to the session, sometimes steering but very rarely directing the counsellor.

This book is a miscellany of supervision stories. I've started with stories about counsellors at the beginning of their careers but, thereafter, counsellors come and go in the book, bringing to supervision a miscellany of different experiences and issues. And because supervisors are established practitioners who draw on their own clinical experience to support (usually) less experienced colleagues, this book also contains a few accounts of my own work with young people, trying to puzzle things out myself, trying to understand the contexts in which young people find themselves and, like my supervisees, trying to respond as helpfully as possible.

For 20 years I've supervised counsellors who work with young people in community settings and in schools; counsellors with lots of experience and counsellors with none; counsellors enjoying the luxury of open-ended relationships and counsellors working within tight time constraints. Those who stick around learn that it's rarely as simple as a young person turning up on time once a week and then going away again. Often, there are other professionals with whom the counsellor must liaise; there are parents or friends of the young person wanting a word. In schools, there are all sorts of contextual issues that have a bearing on the work and must be managed. And then there are the young people who are late. Or don't turn up. Or turn up with a friend. Drunk. And the friend wants counselling…

It can feel like messy work. Counselling with young people involves living with a perpetual sense of inadequacy, knowing that however good the session, many young people will go back to a world in which their parents are absent or don't seem to care, a world full of unfairnesses to which young people must adapt at the same time as they're adapting to all the developmental changes going on in themselves. It's tempting to reach for a manual, to cling to a set way of doing things, to follow the teachings of one particular therapeutic modality.

But with experience comes the confidence to be more adaptable, to live with all the uncertainties, all the impingements. I began my professional life as a teacher, making all sorts of mistakes as I learned to manage formal and informal relationships in and out of the classroom. I became a youth worker, learning how to persuade, how to cajole young people while making a whole new set of mistakes. I ran the school youth centre at the same time as being the school counsellor, negotiating the boundaries as I went along. And for several years after that I ran projects taking counselling into schools, learning to adjust to the cultures and expectations of different schools before settling down to work for many years as the counsellor in one school.

The work doesn't suit everyone. Whether they like it or not, counsellors working with young people are cast as parent-figures more obviously than in work with adults. Because they're older than the young people they're seeing, they readily provoke idealizing or demonizing reactions ('You're the *only* person who understands me!' or 'You've *never* cared about me!'). They have to bear these reactions, understanding them for what they are. But there's also an objective reality: the counsellor really *is* older than the young person; the counsellor really *does* have more experience of life, and young people sometimes need that more experienced perspective. But how do counsellors offer their experience appropriately while continuing to pay absolute attention to the young person's truth, however skewed it may sound? How can they be helpfully authoritative without imposing their own views? How can they develop a therapeutic alliance in which *both* people in the room have a degree of power? How do they resist the temptation of quick fixes when – 99 times out of a 100 – there aren't any? This book explores these and many other dilemmas through the conversations that typically occur in supervision.

2

First Ever Clients

Nikki's already waiting outside my door. 'Help!' she says, half-jokingly, following me into the room. 'I'm in a total panic about what I'm supposed to do!'

We're meeting early in the morning for a bit of preparatory supervision. Later, she'll be a counsellor for the first time, meeting with her first ever clients and, after that, we'll meet up again to see how things have gone.

I tell her that she'll be fine. She's a good student on a rigorous training course. Her anxiety is understandable, though, because until now she's only ever pretended to be a counsellor in role plays with people on the course, and if she wasn't feeling at least a *bit* anxious, I'd be worrying that she wasn't taking the job seriously.

'What do I say? How do I introduce myself? Eeek! Sorry. God, I'm panicking! Don't worry. I'll be all right once I'm in there. But what do you say to them about confidentiality? How do you get the conversation started? Oh god!'

She's never worked with young people before, apart from staffing a few summer play schemes when she was younger. So sitting down with a real young person for the first time will feel very different from sitting down with a role-playing adult. Her mind's gone blank.

'Just behave normally,' I say. 'Explain who you are. Don't say that this is your first morning as a counsellor. Explain about confidentiality and about the times when you won't be able to keep things confidential. Explain what counselling is…'

'What *is* counselling?'

'You tell me.'

'Seriously?'

'Seriously! Let's practise. Imagine that I'm a young person... What's counselling, Nikki?'

'It's a chance to be listened to,' she says, 'to be listened to and not judged. And a counsellor keeps things confidential.'

'What does that mean?'

'It means that I don't tell other people what we've talked about unless you're in danger or being hurt.'

'What if I'm being bullied?'

She looks at me in mock annoyance. 'If you're being bullied... God! Then it depends a bit on what's happening. If you're being beaten up all the time at school or at home, then it wouldn't be fair to do nothing about it. So if something like that was happening, we'd go together and find someone who can stop the bullying from happening...'

'Very good... But Miss, I can talk to most of my teachers already and they're always listening to me. So how's counselling any different?'

'Can you talk to them about things at home?'

'I'm *always* talking to them about things at home!'

She curses. 'I suppose I could say something about empathizing and listening to your feelings?'

'And I'd say that my teachers already do that! So what do counsellors do that's different?'

She's stuck on the difference between being a good listener and being a therapist (Luxmoore 2014). What does a therapist *do* with all that active listening, with all that attunement and empathizing? What becomes of it? What makes therapy therapeutic?

Nikki's not sure.

'Let's come back to that when we meet later this morning,' I suggest, 'otherwise we'll run out of time if we're not careful.

Right now, your job is to make enough of a relationship with the young person that he or she will want to come back again. And try, if you can, to get some sort of family tree, however basic, because most things will stem from family relationships…'

She looks vaguely reassured.

'What's your worst nightmare, Nikki?'

'That they won't want to talk! That they'll hate me and won't want to come back, and then I'll have embarrassed myself and let you down!'

'Just be yourself,' I tell her. 'Be friendly and warm. Don't gush. And be very interested. Get them to tell you the story about whatever it is that's been happening.'

'What if they don't want to talk?'

'Well no one's forcing them to come, so they probably *will* want to talk. But they might find it difficult. They might not be used to talking or they might be shy or scared of telling you things about themselves. So you might have to go slowly, at their pace, respecting their defences, trying to understand. You're a human being trying to understand another human being, trying to understand all the complexities and contradictions and strong feelings and stuff from the past and how angry or sad or frustrated that other human being might be feeling…'

'Okay, okay,' she says. 'I get it! I can do that.'

'And make notes afterwards, so that when we meet at the end of the morning we can try and work out what's important with each person. But, by then, you may already have worked it out for yourself.'

'What do you mean?'

'I mean, keep thinking about what's at the heart of the problem. What's the real conflict inside each person? What's going on developmentally with each person? In a month or in six months' time, what might have changed for the young person because of your meetings?'

At the beginning of any counsellor's career, it's always hard to integrate theory and practice. How do you manage to maintain a perfectly normal conversation while simultaneously thinking theoretical thoughts? How do you go at a young person's pace, respecting his or her defences, when you think you've got a pretty good idea of what might be behind those defences? How do you resist the temptation to give advice? How do you avoid becoming too passive or too active? And what exactly *does* make therapy therapeutic?

Four hours later, she's frantically writing her notes.

She looks up, beaming. 'I've had a brilliant morning! I didn't realize that it would be so good! Or that they'd have so much to say! I've probably forgotten half of it already, which is why I'm scribbling. But it was fascinating! I loved every minute of it!'

I say how pleased I am. 'No problems getting started then?'

'One boy didn't seem to know why he was there,' she says, 'but after I explained a bit about counselling, he seemed happy enough to give it a go, and he's coming back next week. As are the others.'

I'm not surprised. I imagine that any sensible young person would want to talk with someone as warm and enthusiastic as Nikki. Finding an adult who seems to like you and is genuinely interested in your life feels wonderful.

'So the mechanics went well? Explaining things, starting and finishing on time, booking the next appointments…?'

'All straightforward,' she confirms. 'And actually it was pretty easy getting people to talk. I just tried to be normal and it worked! *And* I remembered to ask about their families.'

So far, so good. We need to spend time talking about each of the young people she's seen and developing some sort of working hypothesis about what might be needed with each of them. With no hypothesis, it's hard for any counsellor to know where the conversation might need to go. Simply listening and empathizing, simply being nice to people isn't enough. Young people themselves need to have a sense of where the conversation's going, of what's important…

What's your counsellor like?

All right. She just listens, really.

Is that it?

Pretty much.

So what's the point?

Don't know, really…

I remember trying to supervise a counsellor who wouldn't countenance the idea of a working hypothesis. Whenever I asked what she thought might be going on for the young person, what the meaning of the young person's behaviour might be or what the therapeutic task might be, she replied, 'I wouldn't want to make assumptions'. In some ways this was laudable (not jumping to conclusions, not stereotyping), yet counsellors are always making assumptions, always second-guessing a young person in order to formulate the next question or make the next comment. Sitting passively and letting the young person ramble on without ever daring to give a steer to the conversation often results in young people not coming back because counselling seems too insubstantial, inconsequential, wiffly-woffly. Young people come to counselling when they can't make sense of themselves. They need their counsellors to make sense of things with them and sometimes for them. I'm not suggesting that counsellors should bulldoze their way towards some narrow outcome of their own devising. Of course they listen carefully; they wonder about the meaning of everything; they allow the therapeutic emphasis to shift in the light of new information. But I *am* suggesting that they can't help developing hypotheses and that young people need a sense of direction.

Nikki begins by telling me about a very shy 13-year-old girl whose parents split up when she was six because her father was having an affair with the woman he's since married. The girl has no siblings, hates her pregnant step-mother and says her father is disgusting. She describes her mother (who has no new partner) as sensible and a bit boring.

'Her biggest wish is that her mum and dad will get back together.'

I ask Nikki what she makes of the story, what she thinks it's all about from the girl's point of view.

'Hating her father but also loving him?'

I agree. We also wonder together about what it might be like to have such apparently different parents – one sexual, the other apparently not – and whether these two parents might represent different sides of a 13-year-old girl: a sexually curious part and a sexually shy part, an emerging adult and a retreating child. We wonder about whether young people are always trying to make sense of the parents in their heads and whether wanting a mother and father to get back together sometimes translates as wanting opposite parts of ourselves to be reconciled, re-integrated.

I suggest to Nikki that part of her task might be to help the girl think about the possibility of her parents and of herself as a mixture, no longer simply sexual or asexual, hateful or loveable. We talk about Nikki herself needing to model both sensibleness and expressiveness for the girl.

New information may emerge, in which case Nikki will need to adjust her thinking, her evolving hypothesis, but we have enough of a working hypothesis for her to take into her meeting with the girl next week.

I ask whether there are things she wishes she'd done differently in their conversation.

'I think I might have rushed her a bit,' Nikki says. 'I think I was wanting to inject her with loads of confidence. I liked it when she said she thought her dad was disgusting and I suppose I wanted more of those big feelings.'

'But at the moment she doesn't feel very big?'

'No, and I think I'll have to watch myself in case I get impatient.'

'In case you start trying to make her more like you … ?'

'Ha!' she laughs. 'I'm not confident! You saw the state I was in, first thing this morning! I might act confident sometimes but I'm not really. I'm quite shy.'

I say nothing.

She's thinking about what she's just said. 'Okay, okay! So I might be seeing a bit of myself in her …' She laughs again. 'Bloody counsellors!'

3

Learning to Be Supervised

David has a fountain pen perched in the pocket of his tweed jacket. 'So how do we do this?' he asks, adjusting his chair, trying to get comfortable.

It's our first supervision session and I feel sorry for him. He was a successful antiques dealer before deciding to sell the business and do something different. He's in his mid-fifties now and starting a new career, obliged to become the apprentice having applied to be a volunteer counsellor on placement from his university diploma course. Interviewing him several months ago, I asked why he'd decided to re-train and he told me that there was more to life than making money, that he wanted to make a difference and thought that his experience of life could be useful to others.

My heart sank at the thought of another do-gooder wanting to dish out advice to poor unfortunates. I asked why he wanted to do a placement specifically with young people and in a school.

He admitted that he wasn't sure. 'To be honest, working with youngsters hadn't crossed my mind. But then I thought more about it and remembered my own adolescence and – I don't know – I started getting interested, even though I know I'm completely out of date!'

I squirmed at the mention of 'youngsters'. He'd have to do better than this if he wanted a placement. I asked what it was *exactly* that had got him interested in the prospect of counselling with young people.

'I suppose I was remembering myself as a young man, thinking I knew everything but fearing I knew nothing. And I remember the influence my father had on me. He died when I was 12 and I suppose I missed him when I was growing up, even though I remember him being quite harsh, quite sarcastic and critical. I've no idea whether he'd have approved of the way I've turned out, but I'm pretty sure he wouldn't have approved of someone leaving a perfectly good job to re-train as a counsellor!' David laughed uneasily, checking my reaction. 'In some ways, growing up without a father made me more self-reliant and undoubtedly made me a better businessman, but as you can imagine, there were downsides. And I know counselling isn't about giving people advice – I don't plan to do that – but I suppose if I can be there for some of the youngsters nowadays…'

'Like your father wasn't there for you?'

He took this in his stride. 'I've been attempting to read one of the books on the list, all about loss, which warns you not to try and take someone's place. So I know I can't do that…' He paused, suddenly losing his train of thought. 'Sorry, I don't know why I'm telling you this. I'm not making much sense…'

I was beginning to warm to David, to his awkward sincerity. It was true, he *did* seem out of date, a bit stiff and decidedly uncool in his tweedy jacket, but he also seemed kind and keen to learn. When I offered him a placement at the end of the interview, he seemed genuinely surprised, thanking me profusely as if he'd assumed he'd stand no chance of being accepted onto such an incongruous placement: stiff, middle-aged antiques dealer meets stroppy adolescent. Yet, oddly, it was his lack of presumption, his lack of confidence that I liked.

Months later and we're about to begin our very first supervision meeting. 'So how do we do this?' he asks, the way a teenage son might ask a parent: keen to know but wary of being told.

I sympathize. He's enrolled on a diploma course with people who'll almost certainly be younger, who'll probably be more used to writing essays, who'll understand modern music, modern drugs, modern parlance: people who'll know that referring to teenagers as 'youngsters' sounds patronising. When it comes to antiques and to auctions, then stiff, out-of-date David's the expert, the one with all the experience, and yet when it comes to counselling, he has no choice but to defer to me, worrying all the while that he's left it too late and has nothing to offer the world of counselling. Asking me how supervision works is a perfectly fair question.

'How it works is that we talk about the people you're seeing,' I explain, 'especially the ones with whom you're feeling stuck. Today, as it's our first session, we might say a little bit about everyone, but normally I'll expect you to come having thought about the people you most need to discuss. I'll expect you to bring your notes, not because I necessarily want to see them, but so that you can remember the details about each person. And I'll expect you to make a few notes as we talk, unless what we're saying is of absolutely no interest or unless you've got the most amazing memory!'

'Sounds good!' he says. 'I'm here to learn!'

'And I'll need to make notes as well,' I explain, 'so that I can remember about different people from session to session. And I'll be interested in the *context* of your work, David – in the school staff you're dealing with, in the practical arrangements, in whether there are institutional issues coming up. And also in how *you* are: how the course is going and how the people you're seeing might relate to the things you're reading about and learning on the course.'

'Sounds good to me!'

'And there'll be times when we talk about you and your life, because often the things we get stuck with as counsellors are things which touch us personally or remind us of things we'd rather not be reminded of. So sometimes we'll need to acknowledge some of the more personal things about you and your life. But because this is supervision and not therapy, we'll acknowledge those things; we won't go into them. We'll leave them for you and your therapist to explore in more depth…'

He smiles, keen to please, afraid of getting anything wrong. To pass the course, he must pass this placement, which means that I must be happy with his work. My guess is that there's indignation hidden behind the deference ('Why do I have to go through this process of having things explained to me, of having to learn the ropes? Why can't I just get on with it?'), but we'll leave that discussion until our relationship is more solid. Potentially, I'm another critical parent-figure to be appeased, and so David has reason to be suspicious. I remember his description of his father as sarcastic and critical, so he may well be readying himself to be attacked in supervision.

Today, his first morning, he's seen three young people in the school where we're meeting. In conjunction with various members of staff, I set up the appointments for him and also arranged a room where he could see two boys and one girl, all of them 14 years old.

He opens an impressively large, brand-new, leather-bound notebook. 'So, would you like me to tell you about my first youngster?'

I tell him that 'youngster' sounds a bit patronizing and, yes, I'd like to hear. 'But first, did everything go smoothly, David? Was the room okay? Were they on time? Did they all turn up or did you have to fetch them?'

'They were all there, all on time, though the girl had to leave early because she had a music lesson, but she says she wants to come again next week, so that's a relief!' He anticipates my next question. 'They're *all* coming back next week… Shall I start telling you about Vidal?'

He describes a boy who lives with his mother and sisters and gets into trouble at school. At the start of the day I'd told David to try and get a rudimentary family tree from each person. So he and Vidal have recorded an extensive family tree that he now talks me through, like a police officer briefing a superior. He lists cousins, aunts and uncles, grandparents and parents of grandparents, leaving no one out, no stone unturned in his investigation into Vidal's life. I note down the basics… His father left and re-married when Vidal was eight; his mother has no new partner and has two jobs; his older sister has a boyfriend; his younger sister is 11 and likes gymnastics.

'And Vidal's come to see you because he gets into trouble at school?'

'Apparently so. He says he can't wait to leave school. Says he hates the teachers, especially someone called Mr. Buckland who teaches P.E.'

'Hates Mr. Buckland because…?'

'I'm not sure, but Vidal was very clear that he doesn't like him!'

'Why do you *imagine* that he hates Mr. Buckland?'

David looks perplexed. 'I've no idea. I didn't ask. Sorry!'

'But using your imagination, David…any hunches? Remember that this is a boy whose father left six years ago when he was eight, who's 14 now and living with three women. Pretty tricky stuff if you're a 14-year-old boy. He might be keen to find someone to hate!'

'If you say so…' David looks unconvinced, his deference towards me coloured by confusion, as if he's done his job as a detective, gathering all the facts only to find that his superior is now asking further questions, unfair questions to which he has no answers.

I ask again. 'If you were Vidal…what might you be feeling about your life? Who might you be loving and who might you be hating?'

'I see what you're getting at,' he says. 'You mean Vidal might really be hating his father?'

'Not necessarily, but there might be a part of him hating something. And, yes, maybe Mr. Buckland is a convenient person to hate…'

'He did say that this Mr. Buckland is very hard on them, criticizing anyone in the class who makes a mistake. Apparently Mr. Buckland has his favourites, and clearly Vidal's not one of them…'

David and I could now go in a number of directions. There are Vidal's feelings about his father to wonder about, feelings possibly transferred onto Mr. Buckland as a critical parent-figure in school. There's Vidal's hatred, which will be as important for Vidal as for any young person, hatred that might well be informing his current behaviour in school, leaving him feeling guilty and unable to move on.

I could suggest that David reads Winnicott's 'The Development of the Capacity for Concern' (1963) for more on young people's guilt and need to make reparation. There's also the need for the two of us to be developing some overview of the therapeutic task with Vidal, some sense of where the work might need to go. As with any supervisee, I have an unofficial, part-time teaching role, making pedagogical decisions about how much my student is ready to absorb (Szecsody 1997), about the pace at which David and I can afford to go. And as well as all this, it'll be important that David the apprentice comes away from our supervision meeting with a sense that his first attempts at counselling have been – at the very least – adequate.

There are still two other young people to discuss, so we're pressed for time. But just as I'm trying to decide in my own mind where our conversation needs to go, David takes us off in another direction.

'I must say that I found it hard, listening to him talk about this Mr. Buckland fellow without feeling angry myself,' he says, 'but I know that you're not supposed to get involved as a counsellor, so I didn't really know what to say.'

'Maybe you were picking up Vidal's anger?'

He thinks about this. 'Maybe I was!'

'Maybe you've got quite a lot in common with Vidal…?'

'Not really,' he says. 'I loved sport at school. Couldn't get enough of it!'

'I mean something in common with Vidal about anger, about feeling criticized by authority-figures, about being picked on unfairly…'

He stops and thinks. 'I've never really thought about that, but I do remember feeling like that at his age…' He nods slowly. Then looks worried. 'Is that going to be difficult, if our experiences have been similar?'

'It means that you might be a lot of use to him, David, but that you'll have to be clear with yourself about which are your experiences and which are his. Having similar experiences might give you all sorts of insights into what it's like to be Vidal; you'll just have to be careful about how you use those insights.'

Again he looks perplexed: caught between the relief of being able to relate to his first ever young client, and the fear of what this might mean for a trainee counsellor expected to be calm not angry, adult not teenage. I remind myself that, with a critical father installed in his memory, David will probably also be afraid of being criticized by the placement supervisor sitting opposite him.

Privately, I'm pleased, though. He might be a rather stiff and 'out-of-date' man in his mid-fifties, but it sounds as if his inner teenager is still alive and well after all these years. It's too early in our relationship to suggest that he might be angry with me as well as with Mr. Buckland. I assure David that he's made a decent start and remind him that our time is short; we haven't yet finished talking about Vidal and still have two other young people to discuss.

4

Parallel Processes

'How come you've ended up working with young people, Stephanie?'

'I don't know,' she says. 'I suppose I've always been interested. I've always liked young people and I can remember back to my own schooldays…'

I ask what those days were like.

'Fine… Nothing bad. I was always one of the good girls. I'd never have dreamed of behaving like some of the girls you hear about nowadays. I'd never have been allowed!'

It's our first supervision meeting. I say I'm glad she likes young people because feeling liked by your counsellor is encouraging. But I wonder to myself about her allegedly straightforward adolescence and why people end up working with certain client groups. How much personal investment do we have with that particular group? How much is our work always reparative, always a way of resolving something for ourselves?

In my experience, it's important for counsellors who work with young people to be comfortable with anger. And hatred. And despair. And aloneness. Young people are full of these emotions, and counsellors who've never experienced them (or claim never to have experienced them) are likely to get stuck.

I ask Stephanie what things were like at home when she was growing up.

'All fine,' she says, smiling. 'I never really knew my father because he left when I was young, so it was just me and my mother and then later my step-father and two half-brothers. But obviously they're much younger…'

Suddenly her straightforward adolescence doesn't sound quite so straightforward. 'How are you with anger, Stephanie?'

'Getting better!' she says, smiling. 'It wasn't until I started talking to my own counsellor as part of my training that I realized that I am actually quite angry about a lot of things!'

I remembered running a session for trainee youth workers. They were perfectly okay with the idea of their own anger. Indeed, they were proud to be angry on behalf of so many disadvantaged young people: angry about the government, angry about injustice and about discrimination of every kind. It was when I mentioned hatred that they baulked. I suggested to them that, as well as loving young people, they might also hate them.

Their tutor rounded on me. 'I can honestly say that in all my years of youth work, I've never once hated a young person!'

His students all nodded obediently, hating the very suggestion.

Perhaps I hadn't explained very well Melanie Klein's (1957) idea that the developmental roots of hatred are found in our capacity to love and that the two feelings are entwined. But I was left wondering how they'd eventually get on once they'd qualified as youth workers, once their idealization of young people had worn off and an inevitable degree of disillusionment had set in. How would they bear young people screaming hatred, fighting each other and willfully destroying relationships? What sense would they make of these things? How would they account for the mixture of feelings provoked in themselves as youth workers? Would they take these feelings out on themselves or on their colleagues? Would they decide to give up youth work altogether? Or would these youth workers eventually come to understand their own feelings of hatred as the flipside of love, as inevitable rather than shameful?

Because hatred is so important for young people (Luxmoore 2008), and because young people are so much less practised at hiding it than adults, counsellors have to be aware of their own capacity to hate in order to bear the hatred of young people. I don't expect counsellors to sit there in supervision, seething with animosity, but, as a supervisor, I feel encouraged when I sense that a counsellor still has her own truculent young person shifting around inside her: a young person probably hating one or both of her parents; a young person anxious about sex; a young person with a fragmented sense of self, wondering whether she's worth anything… A qualification in having experienced strong feelings oneself is necessary for counsellors trying to work with young people.

Stephanie begins work, seeing five young people in a school, and we begin meeting regularly at my house to talk about them. A parallel process emerges (Hawkins and Shohet 1989) because, just as most young people in the early days of counselling need their counsellor to be more (rather than less) directive – initiating conversations, structuring the sessions – so Stephanie expects me to call the shots. Typically, she tells me all about a young person and then takes a deep breath, looking up from her notes expectantly, waiting for the answer.

I suspect that, in this way, we internalize and then re-enact for our supervisors something of each client's pathology (Bond and Holland 1998). This can happen with clients of any age, but because most young people are less well defended than most adults, and because the parent–child dynamic implicit in counselling with young people so readily carries over into the supervisor–supervisee relationship, the re-enactment is likely to be more *pronounced* for counsellors working with young people. They're likely to feel more dependent, more dissatisfied, more contemptuous in supervision because these are some of the feelings being stirred up in them every day by young people. So just like a young person, Stephanie tells her story and then expects me to give her the answer, as if she's saying, 'Just tell me what to do!' Other counsellors working with young people might equally well be infuriated by my observations; they might find themselves effectively blurting out, 'You can't tell me what to do!', just like a young person.

For supervisors, the issue of how directive to be never goes away. There are overly dependent supervisees and overly *in*dependent supervisees…just like young people. I've supervised counsellors who hang on my every word, agreeing with everything I say in their anxiety to please, while other counsellors hold back, afraid to say anything for fear of being judged. Still others set me up as the oracle and then become disappointed and angry when I don't have the answers and can't make everything all right. There are some counsellors who tell me everything, barely pausing for breath, unable to discriminate between what's important and what isn't…all of them just like young people.

Stephanie brings to supervision her own adolescent pathology. She's keen to please and anxious about being judged, the way I imagine she might once have felt in her family, hiding any suggestion of anger and keeping her head down with two much younger half-siblings and a new step-father around the house.

She tells me about a girl she's seeing, a girl who apparently says very little, who keeps her head down, seemingly uncomfortable about being in the same room as Stephanie yet still coming back, week after week. Last week the girl picked up the box of tissues on the table and started tearing at it, slowly at first but with increasing ferocity as Stephanie sat opposite, paralysed, trying to decide how best to respond. Eventually the girl stormed out of the room, leaving ripped tissues everywhere.

'I didn't know what to do!' says Stephanie. 'Part of me was thinking it was good that she was showing me how she felt rather than keeping quiet. But at the same time I hadn't said that she could rip up my tissues. It felt like she was attacking me, but I didn't know if I should be trying to stop her. And then when she walked out I didn't know whether to say anything… I've got no idea whether she'll come back next week!'

I say that I doubt if the girl will come back, but that I sympathize absolutely with the dilemma. 'You and I can talk in a moment about what the box of tissues might have represented,' I say to Stephanie, 'but I think the girl was asking whether you'd be able to contain her anger. And I think you said to her that you weren't sure...'

She looks downcast.

I decide that I won't be doing Stephanie any favours by protecting her from the harsh realities of work with young people. 'This is the sort of stuff they don't teach you on counselling courses,' I say, 'and they don't write about it in the theory books. But it's the stuff that makes the difference. "How real are you going to be with me, Ms. Counsellor? If I tell you stuff, stuff about how I really feel, will you be able to cope? Will you be able to contain me or will you be afraid? If I start ripping up your box of tissues, for example, will you tell me to stop, or will you let me carry on, making me feel more and more guilty? And then if I stand up to walk out, will you tell me that you want me to stay or will you just keep quiet? Because if you keep quiet, I won't know what you're thinking and whether you think I should stay or go..."'

I worry that I'm being bullish, telling Stephanie what to do, giving her the answers, but whether we're young people or counsellors feeling small, useless and incompetent, we need someone to take charge and tell us what to do until we feel more confident and able to start doing things for ourselves. I think that the girl with the tissues was asking her counsellor questions and was getting no answers, no containment.

Counsellors sometimes joke that the client is always working on the counsellor's issue. My guess is that the girl with the tissues was working on Stephanie's issue; that Stephanie found herself paralysed in the counselling room because the girl's behaviour tapped into Stephanie's own unresolved (paralysed) feelings of adolescent anger: guilty and uncertain about whether to stay silent and hidden, or to shout and scream, making her feelings absolutely clear to her mother and step-father. Stephanie the potentially decisive, confident counsellor was undermined by Stephanie the indecisive, frightened young person.

'I don't know whether I should tell someone in school that she walked out of our session ...'

Some young people have what Bion (1961) describes as a 'valency', an aptitude for unwittingly picking up and expressing anxieties on behalf of others as well as themselves. They bring to counselling the very anxieties that their families or institutions are struggling with. Stephanie and I can therefore wonder about whether the girl with the tissues might – unconsciously – have been bringing to counselling some of the *school's* prevailing anxieties as well as her own: 'How safe is it for anyone in our school to express anger? Can the professionals in school bear other people's anger? Can women? Is it possible for professionals to be both kind and firm? What would a combination of kindness and firmness look like? How do professionals respond – kindly but firmly – to an angry attack?' I suspect that Stephanie might also have been picking up something on behalf of the school as well as herself, asking me whether or not she should tell other people, as if – through her – the school is now saying, 'We want to be kind but we also need to be firm... How do we do that? And we respect confidentiality, but at the same time we have to know where students are throughout the day. We can't have them wandering the corridors having stomped out of their counselling sessions.'

I've supervised counsellors who've come to supervision with anxieties about whether or not a young person is mentally ill, is suicidal, requires some kind of behavioural intervention; they've come describing young people's anxieties about sexuality, failure, the future, death... It's as if schools themselves regularly get stuck with these anxieties, need supervision themselves and, in the absence of anything resembling supervision, give their anxieties to their counsellor for safe-keeping.

Stephanie looks at me expectantly. Should she have told someone about the girl walking out of the session?

We can discuss the pros and cons of telling someone in the school; I can ask her what *she* thinks; I can tell her that, in my opinion, it all depends… The issue of how directive to be never goes away. As with any young person I might be working with, I wonder to myself how far Stephanie is ready to trust her own judgment. What kind of internal supervisor (Casement 1985) does she have? Does she really need my opinion or is she just deferring to me out of habit?

If there's a sense in which we become like our clients and like our institutions, enacting their anxieties in supervision, then I think there's also a sense in which we become like our supervisors. We watch them carefully; we listen to their words of wisdom; we take note of their attitudes, their mannerisms. We admire them or wouldn't keep going back to see them. We copy them just as young people copy their own role models.

Because of this, supervisors – whether they like it or not – are always modelling styles of and approaches to counselling. As Chapter 6 describes, young people are suspicious of 'weirdness'. Some adults may cope perfectly well with counselling modalities practised in their purest forms, but young people need a relationship that's interactive, mutual and, above all, 'playful' in a Winnicottian sense (see Chapter 18). They need a 'potential' or 'intermediate' space in which to try things out. Stephanie's client brings to counselling a particular kind of stuckness (monosyllabic, head down, avoiding eye contact). My guess is that she needs help in breaking out of that (probably familiar) role, and that the only way she knows is through extremes of behaviour (ripping up tissues, storming out of the room). She needs Stephanie to 'play' with her, therefore, allowing her to try out different behaviours, different roles (Luxmoore 2016). What she gets is Stephanie trying to follow a textbook: never saying anything about herself, asking lots of carefully phrased, open questions, a benign gaze always on the 15-year-old girl sitting opposite her in a room that never changes from week to week.

As her supervisor, I have to model a playfulness for Stephanie in the expectation that our playfulness in supervision will start to inform Stephanie's confidence to be more playful in counselling. If she's a stickler for rules, how can we break some 'rules' in supervision without damaging the process? I remember one counsellor's horror when I offered her a cup of coffee. I remember another being amazed to hear, not that I was going on holiday, but where I was going and who with. I've told counsellors about some of my worst mistakes. I've let slip swear words and political opinions. We've laughed together, cursed together, been interrupted by the doorbell, the neighbour's loud music, the cat.

I make (I hope) a calculated decision about each of these things, especially about whose need is actually being served. Counsellors have to make equally calculated decisions in order to play with young people: decisions that sometimes involve breaking the 'rules'. I like Hurry's (1998) idea of the counsellor as a 'developmental object', assisting young people in their attempts to try things differently. (A counsellor might also serve as a developmental object for a school.) I think that supervisors are often developmental objects for their supervisees, modelling a carefully judged playfulness: a lightness of touch that's also deadly serious.

I can't help thinking that Stephanie's anger will be a key part of her professional development, because anger is what sometimes frees us to break the rules. It's as if the girl with the tissues knows only two ways of living with her anger: one is anxious and defensive (head down) and the other is uncontained and rude (storming out). Neither way is helpful, but learning to operate in the creative space between structure and no structure, directiveness and non-directiveness seems to be the challenge in supervising counsellors who work with young people, just as it is for young people trying to live their lives and for counsellors trying to support them.

The next time I see Stephanie, I ask whether the girl came back.

'She did!' says Stephanie, embarrassed. 'But she was really late for the session. In fact, I'd given up waiting for her and I was actually eating a sweet when she came in. So I offered her one... Do you think that was all right?'

5

Internal Worlds

Angie comes in. She seems quieter than usual. We exchange pleasantries as I make her a cup of coffee.

She settles into her chair. 'I don't know if I've done the right thing,' she begins hesitantly, 'which is why I want to check this out with you…'

I wonder if I'm going to be expected to collude with something unethical.

'You know Lara, who I was telling you about last time? The one with the father abroad?'

I fumble for my notes. I don't remember Lara.

'Well, things haven't got any better for her in school, so I've written to her parents saying that we need to have a meeting – all of us – to sort out what's best for her because it's not really working at the moment…'

Angie loves her job. She loves being able to help young people and loves working in a school, now that she's got used to it. Her clients seem to like her, too; they keep coming back and already the headteacher is talking about trying to find money to buy more of Angie's time.

'So I was with Lara yesterday,' she explains, 'and I asked how she'd feel if I met with her parents. And she didn't really seem bothered, one way or the other. So, obviously, if I *did* meet with them, I wouldn't be on my own. I'd arrange for her tutor to be there and maybe one of the deputies. But I was wondering what you think about meeting with parents because, obviously, you've been doing this a lot longer than I have…'

I like Angie. I like her enthusiasm. She's younger than most counsellors, but is thoughtful and self-critical. I imagine her in 20 years' time: a wise counsellor with masses of experience but still enthusiastic, still passionate about her work.

I skim my notes, trying to remember our previous conversations about Lara, while Angie hovers, wanting to know what I think about this plan to meet with parents who, my notes are telling me, have been separated for nearly ten years. The notes say that Lara's parents don't communicate with each other. Her mother's a lecturer, commuting a long way to the university every day, while her father lives in Geneva and has girlfriends. I've written down one sentence that Lara must have said to Angie at some point: 'I don't expect other people to like me because I don't even like myself!'

I ask more about the current situation, and Angie tells me that Lara isn't doing any schoolwork, has started cutting her arms again and is becoming more and more isolated from her peer group.

'I'm really worried about her. I don't know what else to do…'

Meeting with a young person's parents is a high-risk strategy because there are always unspoken agendas. The young person will often have become the official family problem, masking all sorts of other problems that members of the family won't acknowledge. Family therapy can be a wonderful way of moving things on when there's an impasse, because family therapy starts from the assumption that all problems are family problems; they never belong to one person alone; everyone is responsible and so, in family therapy, everyone is the client. Most meetings with parents in school, however, start from the assumption that the young person really *is* the problem: 'What are we going to do about Lara?' The danger is that Lara's position becomes more entrenched. It can be done, but it takes a very experienced counsellor to prevent this from happening.

Maybe I'll need to find a way of saying this to Angie, but there's a lot for us to think about in the meantime. My hunch is that on this occasion, in her enthusiasm to help, Angie is reaching for a practical solution because she doesn't trust herself as a therapist. She doesn't trust that talking will be enough.

I ask what she thinks is really going on for Lara at the moment.

'I don't know,' she says. 'That's the problem. She's stuck!'

'And what about your stuckness, Angie? The stuckness in your work with Lara? What are the things that don't make sense to you?'

There's never a neat division between our internal and external worlds. Other people and practical circumstances impinge on our emotional lives all the time. So if we're sick or homeless, for example, it's important to address these practical, external realities before beginning to think about the internal worlds of memory and emotion, of unconscious defences keeping anxieties at bay. Counsellors do pay attention to a young person's external world – of course they do. But so do lots of other people – parents, teachers and friends. What many of those people *don't* have is the time and expertise to pay attention to a young person's *internal* world, a world always informing the external one. Like any young person, Lara will be trying to deal with an external world of friends and enemies, of school and parents, a world of responsibilities. But her ability to do this will stem from what's going on for her internally, from the things she's trying to make sense of in her head and in her heart. And that's where counsellors usually need to concentrate their gaze.

I consult my notes. 'The last time we talked about her, Lara was living with her mother who's away working a lot. How's that going?'

'Not well,' Angie says. 'It sounds as if they just do their own thing when they're together at home. And to be honest, it doesn't sound as if her mother has got much of a clue!'

'A clue about how to love her daughter?' I wonder to myself whether Angie thinks she could do a better job than Lara's mother.

'Something like that,' says Angie. 'Lara says she knows that her mum cares about her, but her mum's always busy.'

'Leaving Lara feeling…?'

'Isolated?' suggests Angie. 'Left to get on with it by herself?'

I ask whether part of Lara might also hate her mother.

Angie looks taken aback, but this is important. As I described in the last chapter, we hate because we love. When our love is betrayed or hurt or abandoned, the word we use to describe that feeling is 'hate', and young people hate a lot because they love a lot. I try to imagine the first years of Lara's life, with her parents fighting or shunning or blaming each other until they split up and five-year-old Lara had to get used to living alone with her mother, visiting her father in a new house in Geneva. In similar situations, most young people learn to keep their feelings to themselves for fear of making things worse. All their disappointment, all their rage and sadness and loss, gets put into a box. And the possibility of having *mixed* feelings seems inconceivable because no one ever asks them about having mixed feelings. So some young people find themselves loving one parent and hating the other because it's simpler that way. For many, the feeling of hating a parent becomes an unmentionable, guilty secret to be stored away: evidence of being a bad child. I think of Lara's line 'I don't expect other people to like me because I don't even like myself!' and, as mentioned in Chapter 3, of Winnicott's (1963) description of a young person's need to make reparation, to make up for having hated, to be forgiven for all that's happened. Without opportunities to make reparation, Winnicott argues, young people are left with a sense of themselves as irredeemably bad, condemned to a lifetime of badness. I wonder to myself how far Lara's apparent disaffection at school is a kind of giving up on the possibility of ever being good again and how far her hatred needs to be talked about and detoxified as something inevitable and normal, as the flipside of love.

'I suppose that would make sense,' Angie says. 'But Lara never talks about hating anyone. She doesn't seem bothered about anything.'

'That's the point,' I continue. 'The hatred gets repressed. And keeping it repressed takes up a lot of energy. It becomes a full-time job. Like being depressed.'

Angie looks at me quizzically as if this is all very well, all very theoretical. 'But where does this leave me with her parents?' she asks.

I say that if she's already contacted Lara's parents, then that can't be undone. Maybe they won't want to meet. And if they do, Angie will have to do her best. 'I think you need to trust yourself more as a *therapist*,' I say to her. 'Other people can have meetings with parents and can make those practical interventions, but they might not be so good at helping a young person like Lara with her internal world, with untangling and detoxifying all the unconscious stuff that might be making Lara feel so shitty.'

Angie knows what I mean, but her enthusiasm doesn't yet make up for her lack of confidence when it comes to her own clinical judgments. Like any counsellor, she has to ask herself all the time, 'Where does this conversation need to go? What's it really about? What's at the heart of this young person's problems? What's the anxiety behind the defence? What's the core conflict?' She and I talk about the importance of developing what Bramley (1996) calls a 'dynamic formulation', a working hypothesis, a way of understanding what's going on for Lara *internally*, a way of understanding the therapeutic task. When counsellors are unclear about this and afraid of being directive, the danger is that either they start to repeat themselves, settling for 'listening' and 'empathy' in the absence of any clear therapeutic direction, or they panic and start trying to make practical interventions: inviting parents to meetings, for example. Having a sense of the therapeutic task allows a counsellor to see the bigger picture, to think about what might be informing a young person's behaviour without reaching for short-term, practical solutions that might just as easily be arranged by other professionals.

Angie senses my disapproval. 'I've messed up, haven't I?'

I assure her that she hasn't messed up, 'But I think you probably lost confidence, Angie, and didn't trust yourself to keep thinking about where Lara's behaviour was coming from. It almost always comes back to parents, as you know – the ones in our heads, the ones who give us our confidence or take it away. We're inclined to see the world through these first relationships, loving or hating the things that satisfy or frustrate us. The hating part of us tends to get neglected, though, because other people don't want to hear about it.'

She's emphatically writing notes to herself.

'You're an enthusiastic, positive person,' I say to her. 'What's your hatred like?'

'Wow!' she laughs. 'That's a big question for supervision!'

She tells me how much she hated people as a teenager and how much that hatred is muted now but hasn't entirely gone away.

She stops and thinks. 'So what you're saying is, ask more about hatred. Is that what you're saying?'

As counsellors, we all have our blind spots and we have our reasons for having those blind spots. I suggest to Angie that she might take the subject of hatred to her own therapy.

'Oh, don't worry!' she says. 'I do! I talk a lot about hating people!'

I don't ask.

6

Counselling in Schools

Nikki, David, Stephanie and Angie are all learning to adapt their training to work with young people because, unless they adapt, those young people won't come back. There are plenty of anxious, unsuspecting young people who give counselling a try, only to be greeted with hushed tones, silences, meaningful stares: the clichés of counselling deployed with young people who've come along to find out if they're as mad or as bad as they've been told.

'Hmm, I hear what you're saying,' says the counsellor.

The young person looks bemused.

There's a long pause.

Eventually the counsellor says, 'What I'm feeling is that you're uncomfortable talking with me.'

Another long pause.

The counsellor looks up. 'I'm wondering how you're experiencing our conversation?'

'I'm experiencing it as totally weird!' a young person might say. 'You're either repeating back everything I've just said or you're not saying anything at all! And stop looking at me like that. It's weird! If I want weirdness I can get it from my family. I came to talk about all the stuff that's been happening lately. I didn't really want to come in the first place and I'm definitely not coming back now! You can stick your weirdness up your arse!'

Most counsellors aren't trained to work specifically in schools or with young people. A psychodynamic or person-centred technique might be all very well with consenting adults, but effective counselling with young people depends on adapting that technique to work with nervous, poorly defended, inarticulate young people who don't understand the 'rules' of counselling. They don't know that their counsellor is trying to interpret the transference or trying to be congruent. When they ask, 'Have you got kids?', they don't understand why their counsellor would say, 'Hmm…I'm interested that you're wondering whether or not I've got kids.' To them, that's weird. 'Why can't you just *say*?'

Young people are understandably wary of people who say, 'You can trust me!' They're suspicious of do-gooders. They hate being tricked. Nikki, David, Stephanie and Angie are learning to work with young people but are also learning to work in schools, work which involves demystifying the processes of counselling, normalizing conversations, making what's happening in *and outside* the counselling room as transparent as possible for young people and for staff.

For example, conventional assessments make no sense in a school. 'What am I being assessed for?' a young person might wonder. 'Should I mention the really heavy stuff? Should I cry and swear a lot or should I trust that the counsellor will know what I'm really feeling?' Telling an autobiographical story (see Chapter 11) involves making an attachment, investing in the person listening. So to tell a story and then be told that, after all, counselling won't be possible is unfair to a young person whose earlier attachment experiences in life will already have been difficult. Similarly, referral forms only slow things down and make staff resentful about having to do yet more paperwork. The answer to the question 'How urgent?' is always 'Very urgent!'

Newly arrived in school, a counsellor is unlikely to be given a nice room or even the same room every week. Most schools don't have enough space and, in any case, they want to see if their counsellor is prepared to get her hands dirty before they provide something better.

But there's therapeutic potential in this. The young person will watch how the counsellor deals with these impingements. Does the counsellor panic and curse when the room is double-booked? Or does the counsellor take it in her stride, adapting calmly when things go wrong? Young people will take their behavioural cues from the way they see adults responding to adversity.

The processes of counselling need to be integrated into the everyday life of the school. So in order not to disrupt things too much, the length of a counselling session will depend on the length of a school lesson and, in most schools, a lesson is unlikely to be exactly 50 minutes long. During a lesson lasting an hour or longer, a counsellor might be able to see two different people, but a lot can be done in a short amount of time. And for some young people, fortnightly rather than weekly sessions are fine (Alexander 2012). Sometimes the crisis that brought the young person to counselling passes quite quickly and the young person's anxiety changes: 'Am I still interesting, even without a crisis? Or do I need to keep acting out in school in order to retain my counsellor's interest?' Fortnightly meetings allow the counsellor to see plenty of people but also assure everyone that they're not forgotten, that they're still interesting. Their appointment is booked: they're merely waiting their turn.

When the counselling work actually begins, young people won't simply ask, 'Have you got kids?' They might want to know all sorts of other things. They won't expect the counsellor's life story in all its grisly detail but they will expect a bit of exchange (see Chapter 16). 'Where do you live? What were you like at school? Did you get on with your parents?' These are perfectly reasonable questions deserving of straightforward answers before the focus returns gently to the young person.

And counsellors have to be playful (see Chapter 18). The counsellor with the blank, intense expression only encourages blankness and intensity. Alvarez (1992) describes the counsellor as an 'enlivening object', while Hurry (1998) describes her as a 'developmental object'. Essentially, they're describing a relationship that needs to be interactive, spontaneous, sometimes fun, sometimes light-hearted, sometimes trivial: never monotonously (weirdly) serious. Young people come to counselling because, in some sense, they're stuck and want to get unstuck. They need their counsellor to be (as they would say) 'human', initiating things, trying things out, making some mistakes, playing with them, at least metaphorically. They need their counsellor to be interested in *all* of them: not just in the stuck part.

And they need to know whether and what their counsellor understands. They might ask, 'What do you think I should do?' but they're not really asking for advice: they know perfectly well what to do; that's the easy bit. They're asking for understanding. 'I know I shouldn't have done it, but can you understand why I felt that I had no choice at the time? Given what was happening?' Behaviour doesn't change until it's been understood, *really* understood, and there are times when counsellors need to share their understanding: saying what they think, in effect, rather than remaining determinedly neutral.

Effective counselling in schools also involves sharing the counsellor's wisdom with people outside the counselling room so that everyone in school feels more confident as listeners themselves. The cumulative effect on young people of being in a school that recognizes and values them (or doesn't) is at least as therapeutic (or anti-therapeutic) as any individual work done with a counsellor. That individual work with a young person is always important, but the institution is also the client, and also in need of support. How do key figures in the institution currently contain their anxieties, for example? Does the institution rely on fear and threat? Do people's anxieties spill out endlessly in outbursts of anger, in outbreaks of self-harming, in sexual taunting, in panic attacks, bullying and absenteeism?

Only by working closely with other members of staff can a counsellor begin to have an effect on the prevailing culture in a school. To separate the counselling service from the rest of school life in the name of 'confidentiality' might keep things nice and safe for the counsellor, but it keeps counselling as a furtive and potentially shameful activity where no one knows the counsellor or is allowed to know who's seeing the counsellor. In tough financial times, it's much easier for the headteacher and governors to cut the counselling service they know nothing about and the counsellor they've never met. Disgruntled counsellors can then walk out of the gates complaining, 'This school isn't ready for counselling! They don't really know what they want!', but it's up to the counsellor to educate the school. All schools want magic wands and all schools are disappointed when the counsellor doesn't have one. The counsellor has to accept this and find ways of working with the inevitable institutional disappointment.

So the counsellor starts small. She learns the name of every member of staff. She says hello to everyone by name. She goes into the staffroom as often as possible, chatting to people as part of the vital process of demystifying counselling, making the understandings of counselling available for everyone. Any opportunity to run training for staff is a godsend. Any piece of writing, any time spent explaining the possible meaning of a young person's behaviour is time well spent if it helps staff to understand and support young people better than they might otherwise do. Without this crucial demystifying work, staff won't understand the counsellor; they'll remain suspicious and will almost certainly pass their suspicions on to young people. The idea that young people won't be able to trust a counsellor they see talking to other members of staff is nonsense. It encourages a simplistic split between Who-You-Can-Trust and Who-You-Can't-Trust. The counsellor is there for everyone, for the whole institution. Given time, individual members of staff may themselves want to take advantage of the counsellor's services, but in the meantime they'll be keen to support the work of the counsellor they know, the counsellor they like, the counsellor they trust because they understand what she does, the counsellor who values their own incredibly difficult work, the counsellor who's not weird.

Managing confidentiality in the midst of all this is a skill. Of course, the counsellor keeps confidential whatever's said in the counselling room, but whenever a well-meaning member of staff asks, 'How's he getting on with you? He's been in my tutor group for the last couple of years…' that's where the skill comes in. Counsellors who say, 'Sorry, it's confidential!' and walk off abruptly do themselves and young people no favours. Teachers ask because they care. They want to know if they can help. Most know perfectly well that counselling is confidential: they just want to establish a working relationship with the counsellor. So somehow he or she has to find a form of words that acknowledges and values the teacher's contribution to the student's life without sounding superior, unfriendly or weird.

Because of these complexities, counsellors in schools have to be *more* aware of and *more* adept at managing boundaries than counsellors in private practice. In a school, the counsellor regularly walks past her clients in the corridor. She might have to fetch them from lessons. She might see them around town and they might be keen to greet her. They might tell her things in the playground or in the lunch queue. She might hear about them from other members of staff and sometimes from other clients. Someone's mum or dad or girlfriend might ask to speak to the counsellor… A one-size-fits-all approach to these situations doesn't work. Splitting the private (counselling room) person from the public (outside the counselling room) person is unhelpful in the long run. To a child, things are either completely secret or completely open, whereas young people have to learn that there are degrees of privacy; they have to learn about 'appropriateness': we tell some people some things; we tell other people other things (Luxmoore 2000); we see each other in different contexts and yet we're still the same people. Counsellors in schools have to be flexible, therefore, appreciating the nuances of different situations, working creatively with boundaries and, at all times, avoiding being weird.

Schools are inclined to caricature and pathologize what they don't understand. It's easy for a counsellor in a school, therefore, to convince other people that they're suffering from anxiety disorders and depression, that half the young people in the school are suicidal and that self-harm is the first sign of madness. The level of everyone's anxiety rises and, potentially, the counsellor is set up as the universal saviour – the only one who can really help – while conscientious members of staff are left feeling disempowered. Then when it turns out that, in fact, the saviour hasn't got the answer either, the school loses faith and takes revenge on its false prophet! It's much better to put time into helping people understand that when things go wrong, it's not a disaster; that mistakes are not catastrophes; that bad things do happen in life and that, unfortunately, this is normal: not everyone is suffering from paranoid schizophrenia. Better to suggest that we're all in it together; that no one has The Answer, but that we're all muddling through, using and respecting each other's different contributions; that the counsellor has a unique contribution to make on many levels but is no better or cleverer or more caring than anyone else.

Schools increase the hours of people they trust, people who have earned credibility over a period of time. Having a diploma entitles a counsellor to nothing. Instead, credibility has to be earned the hard way: by being ultra-reliable, by doing great work in a wholly inadequate room, by getting to know the staff, by being fallible like everyone else, by writing clear, interesting reports… And then, little by little, the counsellor's hours increase, a better room becomes available, she's asked to run a short piece of training for staff, and the headteacher has started asking the counsellor's advice.

Counselling in schools is exciting and immensely worthwhile. Potentially, it intervenes with young people of all abilities and social backgrounds before things become more difficult. Potentially, it contributes to a young person's experience of being recognized and valued during *all* his or her time in school, not just in the counselling room but in the daily drip-feed of being in a school that listens, a school that's interested, a school that understands.

7

Institutional Anxieties

I'm waiting for Maggie to arrive for our supervision session and worrying that – once again – I won't be able to offer her anything useful. Sometimes I find myself wondering whether her school really *does* have more than its share of distressed students because, to hear Maggie talk, it sounds as if half of them are starving or cutting themselves while the other half are suicidal. Sitting with her, I regularly find myself feeling helpless in the face of such overwhelming misery and wondering if I've simply led a charmed life. Perhaps I've only ever worked in the easiest schools? Perhaps I'm a fraud? Perhaps Maggie should be *my* supervisor?

She arrives a few minutes late, having been detained, she says, by a last-minute crisis. 'I was just leaving school and a girl rushed up, wanting five minutes. But – and you'd have been proud of me! – I told her that I was leaving and that she'd have to find me tomorrow to make an appointment.' Maggie sighs. 'The trouble was that she immediately pulled up her sleeve and showed me her arm, which was in such a state that I had to do something. So I took her to the school nurse and left them together, which is why I'm a few minutes late. But as you can see, I'm only a *few* minutes late, so I'm getting better!'

I join in with her joke. 'You're getting better, Maggie!'

The joke alludes to the many conversations we've had about counsellors only being able to do so much; about the importance of learning to say no; about the necessity of training and supporting other members of staff to do the job of listening and trying to understand students themselves. I've made the point that most young people would rather talk with the person they already know than with a stranger called 'the counsellor' with whom they have to go through the rigmarole of making an appointment and then waiting for the day of the appointment before finally getting to talk. I've argued that effective school counsellors help other members of staff to become good listeners themselves and that this is as much part of a school counsellor's job as seeing lots of needy individuals (see Chapter 14).

Hearing this, Maggie always nods and says that she agrees, before launching into another story about some young person teetering on the edge of sanity. Sometimes it feels as if she's simply waiting and humouring me while I say my piece before dragging me back into a world in which all young people (according to Maggie) are in the middle of huge crises. At times I feel like saying, 'Haven't you got any normal students at your school, Maggie? Normally upset? Normally confused and pissed off?'

Today, I no sooner ask how things have been than she's off...

'Cherie used to see her father beating up her mother, so it's no wonder that she's the way she is! At school they want her to see a psychiatrist because they think she might have borderline personality disorder, and they're saying they're no longer sure if school's the right place for her. Apparently she ran out of an exam yesterday in floods of tears, saying she wanted to kill herself!'

Already I'm dismayed by the seeming impossibility of everything, but at the same time I know that there are plenty of young people who've witnessed terrible things in their lives. It's not unusual. And I know that schools are always reaching for psychiatric diagnoses to explain the unsettled behaviour of students. It's easy to panic and to pathologize what are often normal developmental crises. 'Borderline personality disorder' might actually translate as 'no longer the sweet girl she used to be'. 'Running out of an exam' might translate as 'walking out of a test'. 'Wanting to kill herself' might translate as 'saying she felt terrible'.

Maggie tells me more about Cherie, looking at me all the while as if to say, 'See how impossible my job is? See the kind of stuff I'm dealing with? I don't suppose other counsellors have to deal with stuff as bad as this!'

I wonder how best to respond. If she's exaggerating, then why? Why does she always seem gripped by panic and so keen to fill me with her panic? I know that there are inexperienced counsellors who do panic when they start hearing about young people's lives for the first time. They hadn't imagined such things happening to so many young people, or the depth of young people's suffering. They panic when they realize how little they can do about it practically and how subtle their contribution to a young person's life will be. But Maggie isn't inexperienced, so why's she doing this?

'I've also been seeing Heather,' she goes on, 'the one whose mother died of cancer. Friend of Cherie's? I can't remember if I told you about her... The one whose older brother abused her? And the father who doesn't want to know? Alcoholic father? Anyway, she's living with her step-mother now, who wants her out and has been phoning Social Services, trying to get Heather taken into care...'

There are schools where the only way to get heard is by shouting loudly. And when that doesn't work, young people turn their feelings into actions as the only other way they know of getting heard. Cutting becomes widespread if that's the only way of drawing people's attention to the fact that something doesn't feel right. If students believe that staff will only react to tears or to an overdose or to someone allegedly 'hearing voices', then those behaviours will make absolute sense to students and become endemic. My guess is that Maggie is working with an institutional problem as well as with lots of individual ones, and that until the institutional problem is solved, she'll continue to be overrun by students catastrophizing and by members of staff panicking.

'I don't know how I'm supposed to find the time to see all these people,' she says. 'I'm already getting in before everyone else in the morning and then staying late. I tell you, they need about eight counsellors at my school!'

I ask what would happen if she was ill.

'I'd come back to an even *longer* waiting list!' she insists, smiling. 'I can't afford to be ill!'

'And yet the fact is, Maggie, that they'd cope. Somehow they'd cope.'

She looks bemused.

'They'd cope because they'd have to cope. The weird thing is that sometimes having a counsellor means that people feel *less* able to cope by themselves. Sometimes they think that the counsellor knows everything and that they themselves know nothing. Sometimes they're more inclined to panic, assuming that you'll always be there to step in and sort everything out.'

She looks at me disapprovingly. 'So what are you suggesting that I do? I can't help it if there's an endless waiting list!'

I find her helplessness irritating, but assume that it's the same helplessness she encounters in school: other people's helplessness absorbed by Maggie and then brought to me in supervision. My job is to contain the helplessness (and my irritation) without getting sucked into feeling helpless myself (see Chapter 8). I can try to understand and offer my understanding back to Maggie as something for her to think about (Bion 1963; Winnicott 1958).

I remind her that we all get stuck in roles sometimes (Luxmoore 2016) and that roles are complementary: if one person gets stuck in the role of helper, someone else is likely to get stuck in the role of helpless person. If the helper moves out of her role, it frees the helpless person to move out of the helpless role and on to a different role. So if the school didn't have its counsellor, other people would step into the role vacated by the counsellor. If Maggie stopped trying to be all things to all people, then other people might be inclined to start taking more responsibility for helping themselves.

'So maybe it would be better if the school didn't have a counsellor,' she says, sarcastically, 'if that's what you're saying!'

I tell her that's *not* what I'm saying. 'A counsellor is a wonderful addition to any school, and they're lucky to have you, Maggie. Counsellors can work with young people's internal, unconscious worlds; they can train other people as listeners; they can model an emotional resilience; they can contribute to the life of a school in so many ways. Schools need counsellors... What I think we're talking about here are some of the *unconscious* processes going on in your school. In the middle of a busy day, we don't necessarily know that they're going on, but if we're able to stop and think and begin to puzzle them out, it gives us more choice about the roles we might usefully play. I think you're probably holding the panic on behalf of the school, Maggie. In other words, they give all their panic to you, all their feelings of helplessness and despair. You internalize these feelings, feeling them as if they were your own and you bring them to me, expecting me to sort everything out, the way people in school expect you to sort everything out...'

She looks deflated, as if she's been told off.

'I think that you simply have to be aware of what might be happening and gently but firmly keep giving people back the responsibility, assuring them that disasters are not about to happen, but that being young *is* scary sometimes and being responsible for young people can also be really scary.'

Her face crumples, tears suddenly welling up. 'I just try to help people, that's all! And it's difficult when I can't!'

She's crying, but I think these are necessary tears: tears for all the sadness in the world, for all the cruelty, for all the things that go wrong, the things that, as individuals, we can do so little about. We may try our best but our best is rarely enough. It's a tough realization.

I ask if she had anyone to support her when *she* was young, and her tears come again.

'Not really! I had to look after my brothers because my mum was ill. So no, there wasn't anyone, which is why it's so hard nowadays when I see so many kids… I don't know…' Her words trail off.

I say nothing. Again, I think this is necessary: finding the link between the work Maggie does now and the adolescence she experienced herself. The more aware she is of this, the more control she can have the next time someone in school appeals to her as The Only Person Who Can Help. Once upon a time, she might well have been the only person who *could* help her mother and brothers, but now, as an adult, there are other people around; she's no longer on her own and no longer has to try and rescue everyone herself.

'I know you're right,' she says, wiping her tears. 'I know I can't do it for everyone. They're just very good at making me feel guilty.'

8

Projective Identification

Sally's been ambushed by the deputy headteacher and two senior members of staff at the school where she runs the counselling service.

'They ganged up on me!' she says. 'They asked me to meet with them but didn't say why. So I went in there, not knowing what to expect. And then, as soon as I'd sat down, they started blaming me for the fact that there's a massive waiting list, saying they can't cope with so many students wanting counselling and how loads of parents are getting angry about it, wanting to know when their child is going to be seen. And they were going on about how one boy's been waiting for counselling for two years! And making out that we keep people in counselling for too long and that we should move them on after three or four sessions. And then asking me if we need to recruit coaches instead of counsellors and whether we should be doing more CBT [cognitive behaviour therapy]...' She sits back in her chair. 'Bloody CBT!'

There's an implied accusation in Sally's story and I feel a familiar anxiety, as if all this is somehow my fault, my responsibility; as if she's saying, 'You're the supervisor who's always telling me to keep seeing people until they're ready to finish! You're the one saying that everyone who wants counselling should have counselling. Well I'm the one who has to pick up the pieces! I'm the one who's getting attacked for doing my job! Or at least, for trying to do my job the way *you* think I should be doing my job!'

I know that she doesn't really think these things. Sally shares my view about democratizing counselling, about short-term work often being a false economy and about the inevitability of waiting lists once young people, their parents and teachers realize that something good is on offer. Which it is: Sally and her team of volunteer counsellors are *very* good.

I suspect that the anxiety I'm feeling is probably the anxiety of the deputy headteacher and her colleagues: an anxiety given to Sally so that they don't have to feel it, and then given to me by Sally so that she doesn't have to feel it. And it'll be an anxiety beginning way back, with anxious young people getting their parents and teachers to feel anxious, and their parents and teachers, in turn, passing that anxiety on to the deputy headteacher and her colleagues.

Unconsciously, we project our uncomfortable feelings *onto* other people, getting them to feel the feelings for us so that we don't have to feel so uncomfortable. In other words, we wind people up. 'Projective identification' (as it's called) is an extremely useful idea, making sense of so much that we find ourselves feeling when we work with other people.

The theory goes that we're on the receiving end of other people's projections all the time, accused of all sorts of things that are untrue. Usually, these unconscious projections bounce off us: we know that we're not really that bad. But the projections stick (we 'introject' them) when we're susceptible to believing these things in the first place. So working in schools and in other organizations, we live with a perpetual sense of inadequacy, knowing that we can't do it for all the people all of the time. When we're accused of inadequacy, therefore, when other people project their own sense of inadequacy onto us, we're susceptible and likely to introject it, feeling the inadequacy as if it was our own.

I suggest to Sally that some of this might have been happening in the meeting with her colleagues.

'I'm sorry,' she says. 'I wasn't meaning to pass it on to you. They were just making me feel that it was all my fault…'

Knowing that we might be feeling other people's feelings on their behalf helps us to take things less personally and resist the temptation to act out those feelings (Obholzer and Zagier Roberts 1994). Sally could panic. She could retaliate. She could take revenge by not talking to anyone at school except her clients from now on. She could resign.

I sometimes think that ideas such as projective identification and 'splitting' should be taught compulsorily to everyone working in organizations such as schools because – unchecked – their effects can be so destructive as people – unconsciously – set about making each other feel wretched. Teachers, for example, are trying to teach lessons at the same time as caring for young people; they're trying to offer firmness as well as kindness. It's very hard to do both of these things at the same time: much easier to do one thing and not the other. Teachers inevitably worry about getting the emphasis wrong and being criticized. So in most schools, there tends to be an unconscious splitting whereby members of staff are characterized (or characterize themselves) as offering one thing rather than the other: 'He's a harsh disciplinarian…' 'She's a touchy-feely pushover…' Schools traditionally distinguish between their 'academic' and 'pastoral' roles, when everyone knows that the two roles are inseparable. It's just that it's much easier to organize things as if the two roles were separate because *then,* teachers imagine, they'll be spared the anxiety of trying to be all things to all people.

In a similar way, counsellors like Sally and her team are trying to care for young people as well as solve their problems. Both tasks are important, but it's hard to do both at the same time. It seems easier to concentrate on only one of the tasks. So counsellors caricature each other and set up ideological battles accordingly: 'He's only interested in self-indulgent, long-term relationships…' 'She's only interested in finding quick fixes…' By the sound of it, the deputy headteacher was accusing Sally of indulging in long-term relationships and Sally – had she retaliated – would have accused the deputy headteacher of only being interested in quick fixes. Both parties would have been projecting their own sense of inadequacy onto the other.

I ask what happened in the rest of the meeting.

'I said that I'd go away and have a think about it,' she says. 'But to be honest, I came out of that meeting feeling so angry! I was writing my resignation letter in my head all the way home. I felt like telling them all to fuck off!'

'And now?'

'And now I've calmed down, and you're probably right – it's their stuff that I'm picking up. It's happened before. I don't know why I didn't see it.'

'Because that's what happens,' I say. 'We don't see it. Projective identification is sneaky!'

'So I need to help them think about their anxieties,' says Sally, writing a note to herself, 'and I need to remind them that there are no quick fixes…'

A fortnight later, she comes back to supervision looking more cheerful.

'It went well,' she reports. 'I went to see Anne, the deputy, but she was busy on the phone to a parent, so I sat there in her office, waiting until she'd finished speaking to the parent. And then all I said to her was something like, "That sounded difficult…" and she was off! Kerpow! About how annoying parents are and how they don't appreciate what we do but still expect miracles and how she feels like telling them to bugger off and find another school! Honestly, she went on at me for about five minutes. It was a tirade!'

'And then?'

'And then she made some joke about how she's the one who ought to be coming to see me for counselling.'

'What did you say?'

'I said I was lucky because I have someone called a supervisor whom I can go and talk to, whereas she and the other teachers don't have the luxury of that. I said that we're all in it together, trying to do our best for everyone without any of us having a magic wand. But as soon as I said "magic wand" she was off again about how the headteacher expects her to have a magic wand and about how he never gets involved in any of the day-to-day crap, just leaves it to her and then complains if something hasn't worked out. So I said about it being tempting for us to take out the aggravation on each other and start blaming each other when it feels too much. And she agreed. We talked about how everyone in the school should be taking more responsibility, not just passing it on to her and the counselling service.'

'Sounds like a good conversation…'

'It was! We were both accepting that it's really hard and that no one has all the answers. She said she really values what the counsellors are doing and how she *does* sometimes expect counsellors to have magic wands.'

'She actually said that?'

'She did! But I haven't told you the best bit… We were talking about tutors doing more themselves and not passing the buck. So I said that they were probably unconfident about what to say to students, unsure about how to listen. And so we've agreed – and this is the good bit – that at the next tutors' meeting, the whole two hours is going to be a session on listening skills which I'll run, getting them to think about the meaning of students' behaviour, plus a bit about mental health, and getting them to practise listening, *really* listening without worrying about having to fix everything and without panicking and sending everyone to Anne or to the counselling service when things can't be fixed…'

Sally sits back and smiles, her own equilibrium and confidence clearly restored. For now.

9

Asking Difficult Questions

Melanie begins to cry, telling me about a 12-year-old boy she's working with, a boy who was sexually and physically abused when he was younger.

'I just don't understand how anyone could do something like that to a child,' she explains, weeping. 'My son's the same age now as Stuart was when it happened. And when I think of anything like that happening to my son ...'

She tails off, overcome. I wonder to myself why she wants to discuss Stuart. Is her work with him stuck in some way or does she simply need to share with me the horror of his abuse? Was Melanie herself abused as a child?

I ask what she thinks Stuart needs from her.

'I don't know what anyone needs from a counsellor in that situation,' she says, wiping her eyes. 'Or what any counsellor could offer that would make the slightest bit of difference!'

In a sense, she's right. Counselling doesn't change anything that's happened. But counselling can help us to bear whatever's happened without it interfering so powerfully in our lives. I could ask Melanie to think of her own worst experience in life and what she herself would have needed from a counsellor in the aftermath of such an experience. But she's too upset at the moment. A question like that wouldn't help.

Sometimes counsellors have to steel themselves and listen to terrible stories, knowing that this is the best they can offer.

Sometimes in supervision there's nothing to say, only a need to witness the counsellor's experience as the counsellor has witnessed a young person's. 'You can only do what you can do,' I find myself saying rather pathetically to counsellors struggling to bear the weight and complexity of the world's problems, wishing they could do more.

Still I'm surprised that Melanie's upset. Surely she knows that these things happen, that some adults hurt children, that the adults who are supposed to look after us often do us the greatest damage. But I remember my own supervisor once pointing out to me that I was inclined to take a rather benevolent view of the world, a view that might be blinding me to the nature of some people. 'Remember that people can be absolute shits!' she said. 'There's nothing wrong with trying to find the good in people as long as you remember that the same people who can be good can also be very bad!' Years later, I remember listening to asylum seekers describing the torture and killing, the endless capacity of human beings to inflict cruelty on one another. I remember listening to their stories and thinking, 'Actually, in certain circumstances and under certain pressures, I'd probably be capable of doing equally terrible things. I might like to think of myself as a loving person, a fair person, but if I'm honest, I'd probably be capable of joining in and inflicting all sorts of cruelties myself.' Acknowledging my own potential to be cruel somehow helped me to bear the stories without running away.

'It's hard, listening to all the horrible stuff,' I say to Melanie rather feebly, attempting to get her talking again. 'And sometimes there's nothing to say, nothing to do. As counsellors, we just have to bear it with the young person...'

She nods. 'When Stuart was telling me what happened, I didn't know what to say. I wanted to say I was sorry but that sounded too pathetic! So I ended up asking him about how he was feeling now. And as soon as I said that, I knew I was just running away. I was trying to find a way of stopping him talking about the abuse itself, so that I wouldn't have to listen to any more of what he was describing.'

I point out to her that people don't always need to go over the details of what's happened. Sometimes they do and sometimes they don't: it's a clinical judgment for the counsellor to make, gauging the other person's need. 'But on this occasion, you thought you were running away, Melanie?'

'I couldn't see the point,' she says. 'I couldn't see what was to be gained by going over it. He's told social workers; he's told the police. Why would he need to tell me?'

I agree with her that there's no point in simply going over and over old ground. 'But I suppose if he's never told *you* before and if you're going to be important in his life, then he might well need to tell you at some point. And when that point comes, you have to bear it with him, remembering that there was no one to bear it with him at the time when it was happening.'

'It feels wrong, though,' she says, 'asking a 12-year-old boy to tell me about the terrible things that have happened to him.'

I share her concern. 'It can be wrong,' I say, 'if it risks re-traumatizing him, making him re-live the experience. There's absolutely nothing to be gained by that. It reminds me of all those clichés about how people are supposed to use counselling to get in touch with their feelings. As if getting in touch with your feelings was an end in itself. It isn't! Getting in touch with your feelings is the easy bit! The hard bit is what you *do* with those feelings. What's the point of feeling afraid again? Or paralysed? Or furious? How's that supposed to help a 12-year-old boy?'

'Exactly,' says Melanie. 'That's what I was thinking...'

'And yet sometimes it's important that the story is told and is witnessed by another person. "This is my truth... This really happened to me..." It can be really important for a young person to have that affirmation. And sometimes it's important to re-tell the story in order to do it differently – to say the things that couldn't be said at the time, to look back at what happened from a different perspective, no longer a helpless child but looking back now an older boy, better able to understand. I imagine that, for Stuart, one of the most important things will be that – this time, with you beside him – he remains in control, stopping the story when he needs to stop it, angry when he needs to be angry, sad when he needs to be sad, telling you as much or as little as he chooses, staying in control this time.'

'But I always worry about saying the wrong thing,' says Melanie. 'I hate the thought of making anything worse. I'd never forgive myself.'

'So ask him,' I suggest. 'Ask Stuart if it's okay to talk about this. Ask if he's happy to say more. Make it clear that the conversation is entirely on his terms. He can stop the conversation at any time. He can say no.'

'But some abused children have learnt to please adults,' she says, 'so what if he's just trying to please me?'

'Is he?'

'I don't think so,' she says, pausing, thinking about it. 'No, I don't think so.'

We're both silent.

I remind her of the connection she was making with her son. 'Has anything ever happened to him?'

'No,' she says, 'no, but he's getting older and wants his independence and I can't be with him all the time.' Briefly, her tears come again, then subside. 'It's also hard,' she says, 'when you want to get hold of the people who do these things to children and…I don't know.'

'And kill them? And take revenge on them? And lock them up?'

'I suppose so,' she says, 'except that, as counsellors, we're not supposed to want to do things like that. We're supposed to be non-judgmental!'

Melanie's passion and compassion will be at the heart of her effectiveness as a counsellor. I say I doubt whether it's ever possible to be non-judgmental. 'Have you told Stuart that you think what happened to him was wrong, that it wasn't his fault?'

She shakes her head.

'Well tell him, the next time you see him. And don't worry about that being a judgmental thing to say. It is! But my guess is that it's what he most needs to hear from you.'

She smiles, no longer tearful. She asks if I think young people ever really recover from the harm done to them.

I ask what she thinks.

'I hope they do,' she says, 'at least in part, or we wouldn't bother doing our jobs. I think we make a difference. It's just hard sometimes…'

10

Dependence and Independence

'He hasn't turned up for the last two weeks,' says Alison, 'and hasn't been in touch, so I don't know whether to phone, or wait and see if he turns up this week.'

She's also not sure whether her counselling agency has a policy about contacting young people out of sessions.

I suggest that she phones Carlo as soon as possible, rather than sit for another hour later in the week, twiddling her thumbs, waiting to see if he arrives. In my experience, there are plenty of young people who miss sessions almost deliberately to see if they'll be chased. 'How much does my counsellor really want to see me? Having wasted her time, having made her life difficult by not turning up, will she still want to see me? Will she make the effort?' For many young people, ambivalent about counselling in the first place, it's a test to see if their counsellor will give up at the first sign of trouble like other professionals have done in the past, thereby proving what the young person always suspected, that no one really cares. Young people are partly hoping that their suspicions *will* be confirmed, that the world really *is* out to get them, but they're also secretly hoping that this latest professional will persist: phoning, texting, visiting if necessary… whatever it takes.

Understandably, adults want to encourage young people to be more independent, to take more responsibility for themselves, but there's always a part of any young person longing to be dependent, longing for someone else to take the responsibility. Young people are always on a developmental continuum enacted in counselling relationships as they swing back and forth between dependence and independence: at one moment helpless and wanting their counsellor to tell them what to do; at the next moment distant and insisting that they know best.

Like a child invited to do something she suspects is naughty, Alison looks extremely doubtful about contacting Carlo.

I ask if her own counsellor ever contacted her out of sessions.

'Never! But she didn't need to, because I never missed a session.'

I remind her that most young people aren't as well organized or as well behaved as adults, and that counsellors working with young people usually have to adapt their practice, becoming much more proactive. Lomas (1987) argues that therapists must first learn the rules in order to decide how and when to break them. So if Alison has learned a rule that you sit waiting and avoid contacting people outside sessions, then there are times when things have to be done which stretch the therapeutic frame in order to preserve the relationship: there are times when the rule has to be broken.

'Actually, she did contact me once,' Alison remembers. 'One week she was ill and she phoned me to cancel.'

'What was that like?'

'Fine! I felt sorry for her, being ill.'

'And how was it when you met again?'

'I remember feeling a bit peeved,' Alison says, 'because when I asked if she'd had a cold, she wouldn't actually tell me. She went all secretive, and it felt as if I shouldn't be asking, as if I was being put in my place. After that, we went back to being counsellor and client again.'

'A relief or a disappointment?'

'Both, really. In a way, a relief because I could go back to just thinking about myself, but in another way it was disappointing because I couldn't see the harm in her telling me if she had a cold.

I'm not a child! But she was probably thinking it was some sort of boundary issue.'

'She might have had something worse than a cold…'

'Exactly! And that's what I started thinking, that she might have cancer and that sooner or later she'd tell me and we'd have to end.'

'But you didn't ask?'

'No, because of the boundaries thing. I knew she wouldn't tell me if I did ask and that I'd just end up feeling stupid for asking!'

'Like a child?'

'Just like a child…'

Alison is describing a confusion of dependence and independence, of being expected to remain a child while desperately wanting to know what the grown-ups know. Maybe her counsellor judged that any information about the illness was more than Alison was ready to bear. And maybe the counsellor's judgment was right. Maybe there were all sorts of transferential reasons why telling Alison about the illness would have set things back therapeutically. But had Alison been a *young* person and had she been less robust, she might well have felt shamed at being rebuffed in this way by her counsellor and might have retreated altogether.

There are some young people on the dependence–independence continuum who are ready and others who are not ready to live with different kinds of information about other people. Counsellors have to make judgments about this all the time, as Alison herself must now make a judgment about whether or not to intervene with Carlo. How much is his silence an expression of dependence ('Please come and get me, Alison! I'm stuck and don't know what to do!') and how much is it an expression of independence ('I don't need you any more, Alison! Leave me alone! Go away!')? How much is a young person's apparent independence ('I don't need you any more, Alison!') sometimes a cover for a dependence that's too shameful to acknowledge? 'Actually, I desperately need you, Alison, but my need makes me vulnerable. My desperation is embarrassing. So it's better if I stay away from you and don't come back to counselling…'

However feisty, however unconcerned young people may appear to be, many come to counselling wanting to be looked after. As if anticipating attachment theory, Winnicott (1967) describes the good fortune of some children who have 'introjected reliability'. Having never been significantly let down in their lives, they see the world and the people in it as essentially reliable and trustworthy, whereas less fortunate children have never been able to take anything for granted and have long since given up searching for reliability. Occasionally, they might experience a 'regression to dependence' whereby they let go of their battered independence for a while and risk depending on someone, hoping that he or she will prove reliable. I suggest to Alison that counselling might have been Carlo's experiment with dependence. He might have tried it and decided that he simply couldn't bear the experience of needing another person.

'But we were getting on well,' she says, 'or at least I thought we were. Not coming back and not even bothering to contact me doesn't make sense.'

I ask whether his absence might be regressive, the behaviour of a 16-year-old 'child' still searching for reliability, a child lost and hoping to be found. For some young people it's upsetting to meet someone who's kind and who cares because it's a reminder of something they've never had. Winnicott (1962) observes that a baby might never be able to connect with a mother's goodness yet senses that it's always there, tantalizingly out of reach. Understandably, the baby might therefore choose to destroy so tantalizing and persecutory a relationship. Counselling with Alison might have reminded Carlo of something he'd never had, something too tantalizing, too painful to risk. Murdin (2000) describes a client ending suddenly and unilaterally as '…an attempt at total control. Either the therapist has to be eliminated, or those parts of the self that the [client] cannot tolerate must be silenced by ending the therapy that threatens to give them a voice' (p.62).

'But if I contact him, won't I just be acting into his fantasy?' asks Alison. 'If I chase after him, I'll be implying that he can control me when, in fact, he can't. Surely he has to get used to the frustration of not being able to control his parents and other parent-figures in his life like me?'

She's right. Learning to bear frustration is a developmental priority for young people as they try to live with the world as it is rather than as they'd like it to be (Phillips 2012). So pandering to a young person's narcissism won't help, and yet there's nothing to be gained by losing Carlo without first trying to find him. Alison could sit in her room, taking his apparent expression of independence ('I don't need you!') at face value, waiting for him to make the first move. And then, when he can't make the first move because it's too shameful, the relationship would end. She'd be left wringing her hands, blaming him for the fact that he couldn't take responsibility for the situation himself by asking to re-start counselling.

'You're right about frustration,' I say to her, 'but unless I've misunderstood, Carlo isn't some pain-in-the-arse teenager expecting to get things his own way. He sounds more like a baby who's never known reliability.'

His parents split up when Carlo was two, Alison explains, after which his mother was obliged to work away from home a lot, leaving Carlo to be looked after for days on end by his mother's parents nearby. When he was 12, his grandfather died, and now, four years later, Carlo is still living with his mother who still comes and goes, depending on her work. He still goes to visit his grandmother sometimes.

I ask Alison why Carlo came to see her in the first place.

'Apparently it was his doctor's idea because he wasn't sleeping, wasn't going to work, and on some days, wasn't even leaving the house. Since he left school last summer he's been working in a pizza place, making dough. Or at least, he *was* working there. The last time I saw him, he reckoned he was about to lose his job.'

She and Carlo have met three times. I ask what he's like.

'Nice guy,' she says. 'Quite funny. Quite articulate. He seemed pleased to be coming to see me and was very definite about wanting to keep coming.'

'To keep you happy?'

'Maybe…' She sounds irritated. 'I'm sure you know more about these things, but at the time I thought he seemed genuinely pleased to continue.'

'So what's your guess?' I ask. 'That he can't be bothered? That he keeps forgetting? That he's got a better offer from somewhere else? I'm simply wondering if his attendance was ever straightforward. He sounds like someone who might have developed an ability to keep people happy but who, underneath, might always have been pretty unsure about himself. And I wonder whether that uncertainty might be catching up with him now that he's older…'

She looks blank.

'What I mean is that staying at home and not coming to counselling might be a kind of regression, like going back to some sort of little-boy experience, hiding away in a room. Presumably if you're a small child, if your father's left home and your mother's away working a lot, you have to get good at looking after yourself… And maybe over the years Carlo's become very good at looking after himself but doesn't want to do that any longer? Maybe he's always known that something's missing? That there's something out there?'

'Like what?'

'Like that introjected reliability thing, that experience of being able to take people for granted. Maybe he's had to perform, learning to be nice, funny, articulate Carlo because he's never been able to take anyone for granted? I imagine that if you've never been able to rely on anyone in your life, you could end up feeling pretty alone… You might have had two really nice grandparents but then, when one of them dies, you're reminded that the other will also die and that, sooner or later, you'll be on your own again. But at least your aloneness would be familiar, whereas the prospect of being with someone potentially good, like a counsellor, would be tantalizing and therefore really, really scary.'

'So you think I should get in touch with him?'

'Absolutely! The worst that can happen is that he tells you to piss off…'

'I'm not sure I want to be told to piss off!'

I assure her that if she's going to continue working with young people, then being told to piss off goes with the territory. 'Not coming back to counselling might be part of the issue, part of the therapeutic task. How do you help a boy who's never been able to depend on anyone risk doing so without losing his sense of independence? It's what Glasser [1979] calls the "core complex" at the heart of everything. Glasser says that we're always lurching between merger and separation, dependence and independence, like a toddler moving away from its mother but always looking back to check that she's still there. Remember Winnicott's [1971, p.114] line about "When I look I am seen, so I exist"? Maybe Carlo's never really felt seen, and maybe, because of that, he's afraid of what it would be like to be seen…'

'Or maybe I'm just a crap counsellor!'

'Which is what his mother might say! "Maybe I'm just a crap mother? Maybe that's why my 16-year-old son keeps his distance from me? Maybe he knows that if I go near him, I'll see his aloneness, his rage, his despair. I'll see that – underneath everything – he's really a child…"'

Alison looks unimpressed.

'What does Carlo actually say about his mother?'

'Nothing bad. Just that she's away a lot. But apparently they get on fine when they're together.'

'Even so, it would be interesting to know what it was like between them when Carlo was younger. I'm imagining his mother coming back from working away somewhere and finding her son either screaming blue murder or slumped in a corner, refusing to have anything to do with her. Or grabbing hold of her and refusing to let go. Or doing all of these things at various times… It might have been hard for her to know how to respond.'

'If you say so!'

Alison sounds fed up with my hypothesizing. I ask what she's thinking.

'I'm thinking that men theorizing about what it's like for mothers makes me uneasy.'

'Because men don't know what it's like for mothers?'

'Because it's never men who get blamed for going to work! It's never men who have to feel guilty about leaving a child!' She glares at me. 'It's not you who's got to contact Carlo and it's not you who's probably going to get told to piss off!'

'You're right,' I splutter, taken aback. 'It's you who has to deal with the situation. It's you who has to take responsibility for what happens next.'

She says nothing, fuming.

'Does that sound familiar, Alison?'

She shrugs, giving nothing away.

We pause, both taking stock. I'm frantically trying to work out what's just happened. She may well be right about men thinking they know what it's like to be women, but it's a cheap shot. Alison's hostility is probably informed by something more personal. Maybe she identifies with Carlo's mother? Or with Carlo? Maybe supervision puts her in a position of dependence where she's obliged to come and listen to me pontificating, and maybe that revives old resentments about certain kinds of men? Grinberg (1997) writes of supervisees for whom 'envy can be so regressive that they cannot stand the other person having knowledge that they lack, and therefore they try to destroy the supervisor through insidious attacks' (p.11). Alison's attacks aren't insidious, but if counsellors are always gauging where young people are on the dependence–independence continuum, then supervisors must also be gauging where their supervisees are on the same continuum. How much does Alison need my pontificating and how much does she need to be left to decide things for herself? And if the answer is that she needs different things at different times, then what does she need right now?

I ask.

She hesitates. 'I don't know. Part of me wants to leave Carlo to make up his own mind, but part of me knows that you're probably right and that I should contact him…'

I say it's always hard to know what to do and what to feel when young people don't turn up.

'Oh, I know perfectly well what I feel!' she says. 'I'm pissed off with him, the little shit!' She laughs at herself. 'Of course, I don't *actually* feel that, but you know what I mean! I'm the one who's sitting there, waiting for him, wasting my time when I could be doing something useful.'

'Instead of being made to feel useless?'

She looks at me suspiciously, as if I might be suggesting that she herself is useless. I want to remind her of Winnicott's (1958) paper 'Hate in the counter-transference' about the inevitability of a therapist's hatred. I'm pleased that she can call Carlo a 'little shit', presumably in the knowledge that I *won't* be condemning her as a bad counsellor.

Counsellors bring to supervision the same anxieties about dependence that young people bring to counselling. For most, the prospect of being reliably dependent on someone is tantalizing, but for some it feels like regressing to an anxious, unreliable past. And yet counsellors have to allow themselves to be supervised without fear of being diminished. Kernberg (2012) writes that 'One important aspect of the experience of dependency…is the capacity to let oneself be taken care of by the other without suffering from a sense of inferiority, shame, or guilt' (p.284). This is easier said than done when it comes to supervision. Counsellors depend on young people in the same way that all sorts of other people depend on their jobs for validation, for a sense of worth. When a young person like Carlo doesn't turn up, therefore, counsellors and supervisors can speculate about what might be going on for that young person, but for the counsellor it always feels personal, like loving a child who refuses to be loved. The counsellor hates the child's rebuke and might hate the supervisor to whom she must go and talk about the rebuke.

My guess is that Alison has some sense of what it might be like to be Carlo's mother, wanting to make things better for her son but frustrated by his ambivalence about engaging; angry with men who don't get involved yet presume to give advice. Men like Carlo's father, perhaps. Or me.

We meet again, two weeks later, by which time she's phoned Carlo.

'He was very apologetic. He said he'd forgotten and then he'd got the times muddled up. To be honest, I didn't really believe him, but we arranged another session and finally met up yesterday.'

'And…?'

'And it was all right. We had a decent session, but we're not going to meet again.' She checks for my disapproval. 'We didn't really talk about why he hadn't been coming to counselling. Instead he talked about losing his job at the pizza place and about how he wants to join the army. I didn't really say much. I just let him talk. You'd have been interested, though, because – twice – he said that being in the army was a 'reliable' job and I could hear you going "Ah, ha!"'

'Like the smug bastard that I am?'

She smiles.

11

Developing Autobiographies

Once counsellors have become more experienced, they often find themselves supervising less experienced counsellors. But their own counselling work doesn't stop. Like other supervisors, I continue as a counsellor myself, attempting to make sense of young people, just as the young people I'm seeing continue their attempts to make sense of themselves.

Travis is 14. 'I'm here because everyone keeps having a go at me,' he says, sitting down for our first meeting. 'I've had enough of it! They all reckon I've got anger management but I haven't. I just need them to get off my back and leave me alone!'

Plenty of young people come to counselling feeling persecuted: persecuted by the bullies in their schools, by the critics in their heads, by the unfairnesses of life. They have plenty of reasons to feel persecuted.

Travis explains that, because of his angry behaviour, he's about to be expelled from school. 'I've always been a mouthy little sod. That's just the way I am. If someone wants to know what I think, then I tell them!'

Bullies, critics and unfairnesses are the obvious persecutions. What's harder for young people to describe is the feeling of being persecuted by a story: a story from which there's no escape, an autobiographical story in which a young person like Travis is cast as 'a mouthy little sod' and then expected to behave accordingly because that's the script, that's the way story goes, 'that's just the way

I am'. Phillips (1994) writes that people come to therapy because 'the way they are remembering their lives has become too painful; the stories they are telling themselves have become too coercive and restrictive'. One of the aims of therapy, he writes, is 'to produce a story of the past – a reconstructed life-history – that makes the past available, as a resource to be thought about rather than a persecution to be endlessly re-enacted' (p.69).

We're imprisoned or liberated by our stories. They always have a bearing on the way we behave and how we feel about ourselves. In other words, *who* we're supposed to be affects *how* we're supposed to be. If people have always told Travis that he's 'a mouthy little sod', then he's likely to behave the way he imagines mouthy little sods are supposed to behave. He becomes that person because, as he says, 'that's just the way I am'. And at the moment, his story of the 'mouthy little sod' is doing him no favours, repeatedly getting him into trouble.

So how do counsellors help young people like Travis develop less imprisoning, more flexible autobiographies? How do we encourage young people to understand and be interested in their own stories and in themselves? How do we help them to stop and think about themselves rather than impulsively act out their anxieties, sometimes with disastrous results?

His mother has been with her partner since Travis was ten years old. They have two children, Albert and Victoria. 'But they're just little kids,' says Travis. 'I'm out of the house most of the time so I don't really see them.'

I ask about the earlier part of his life.

He can't remember much. His parents split up when he was about two years old, and for a few years his father sent him money at birthdays and Christmases. But then he stopped. 'I think he might live in South Africa or somewhere like that now. His mum still sends me a card at Christmas. But to be honest,' says Travis, 'I don't know why she bothers. She lives in Glasgow. I've never even met her. She might be his mum, but she's nothing to me!'

We all have an autobiographical self: a story that looks back, trying to make sense of our lives. It might be a story idealizing or demonizing various relationships in our lives, a story leaving out certain experiences we'd rather not remember, leaving out certain parts of ourselves that we'd rather not acknowledge while highlighting others. We recount different chapters of the story to different people at different times, according to how we want to present ourselves: as the victim or as the conqueror, as the neglected child or as the brave warrior, as the persecuted teenager or as the eternal peacemaker…

Young people usually tell black-and-white autobiographical stories about good guys and bad guys, fairness and unfairness, blame and responsibility. They tell grandiose or helpless stories; stories squeezed into narrow, self-justifying shapes; stories always serving a purpose, simplifying life when life feels too complex to bear; stories offering certainties when everything else seems horribly uncertain. I remember another young person, Sandra, whose story was evidently entitled 'I Was Never Wanted' because that's how she thought of herself. That was the simplicity she was holding on to. Bobby would probably have called his story 'Nobody Understands Me'. Jamilla insisted on a story called 'I Don't Care', while Leon's autobiography would have been called 'Never Trust Anyone'.

Every story is doing a job, protecting the young person in various ways. It becomes familiar and keeps the young person safe until, eventually, it start to imprison the author with its simplicities.

With support, young people like Travis can become better able to bear complexity and nuance, developing more flexible stories with new titles, stories taking account of mixed feelings and mixed motives, stories that are less persecutory. Thinking with me about her life, Sandra's old, simplified story, 'I Was Never Wanted', changed subtly and became 'I Was Loved, But By Unreliable, Inconsistent Parents'. For Bobby, 'Nobody Understands Me' became 'I Keep Things Hidden From Other People Because I'm A Mixture Of Good And Bad Qualities'. Jamilla's autobiography which was originally called 'I Don't Care' became 'I Do Care But When I Was Younger I Was Too Angry To Let People Know', and Leon's 'Never Trust Anyone' became 'Sometimes The Price Of Loving People Is Getting Hurt By Them'.

Stuck with an imprisoning, out-of-date story, young people are only able to move on once their old story has been understood by other people: how the story came to be, why it made sense at the time and why it no longer serves its purpose. So my first and most important job is simply to understand something of Travis's life.

I ask about the early years, about how his mother and father came to be together.

He knows nothing. 'But it's like my mum says, the past is the past and you can't change that. It's just boring, really. All that. You've got to get on with your life…'

'Any idea how they met?'

He shakes his head.

'How old was your mum?'

'She's 33,' says Travis, not wanting to risk the maths.

'So she was about 19 when you were born…'

He shrugs.

'And your dad?'

'No idea!'

'Older or younger?'

'Older, I think… because he'd been in the army or something but apparently he got kicked out.'

'So she was about 19. Left school. Probably working somewhere… And he was maybe in his early twenties when they met?'

'Maybe,' says Travis. Then adds, 'I'm not being rude or anything, but why are we talking about this? I've come here about my anger, not about my mum and dad!'

It's a fair question. Instead of me giving him a simple answer to his troubles ('Why don't they get off my back? Why can't they leave me alone?'), we're wondering about the early years of his life.

I could say to him that it's hard to know who we are if we know little about where we come from. I could say that if the first chapters of our autobiographies are missing ('Who my mum and dad were… How they came to meet… What they were like together…'), then it's as if the very foundations of our lives are missing. But he'd dismiss this as psycho-speak, gobbledegook.

'The reason we're wondering about your mum and dad is because we don't know much about them. And love them or hate them, our parents are always important in our lives because that's where we start from. The way we feel about our lives and the way we deal with people nowadays is always – or at least, sometimes – to do with the way we feel about our parents and about the other important people in our lives.'

'But I still don't see the point of asking about my dad!' he says. 'I've told you, I haven't seen him for years. I don't think about him. He might as well be dead for all I care!'

'And if he was dead, what would you be saying at his funeral?'

'I wouldn't be going to his funeral!'

'What would you be saying in your head?'

'I'd be saying that he's a total loser! That I'm better off without him! But I've told you, I don't think about him…'

I risk losing Travis if I push any harder. The simplicities he's constructed around his father ('loser…better off without him') are there for a reason, protecting him from any feelings of loss or longing or from any curiosity. I need to respect his defences and what they conceal.

'He's a loser who's never really been in your life and a loser you've managed perfectly well without…'

'Exactly!' says Travis, grinning, pleased that, at last, his counsellor has finally understood something.

'A loser you never think or wonder about…'

'No!'

'And a loser your mum doesn't think about either, ever since she stopped loving him in the years after you were born.'

'Exactly!'

Developing a new autobiographical story is like developing a new identity. It takes time; it can be scary and there will always be remnants of the old story. The fact that his father has been absent for most of Travis's life isn't going to change, but we might eventually be able to think together about the identity of the man his mother once (probably) loved, about what their lives were like in the years before and just after Travis's birth, about what led to their separation and about how they might each be thinking about their son nowadays. We might be able to open up some of these autobiographical strands without Travis getting scared.

'I can see why you wouldn't want to think about him,' I say. 'After all, you've survived perfectly well without him for the past 12 years; he's not involved in your life at the moment and, as far as you're concerned, your life's complicated enough without adding a whole load of extra hassle!'

Travis looks reassured. All we're doing is respecting his defences, his refusal to think about his father, but that's important, acknowledging that he's not stupid and that his defences make absolute sense, even if they're probably what get him into trouble when he falls back on 'mouthy little sod' as the only way he knows of dealing with situations. We have to move on from the stock story of 'mouthy little sod who says whatever he thinks' to find new stories, new versions of Travis capable of adapting to situations. But we also have to acknowledge the usefulness of 'mouthy little sod' over the years and its usefulness now as a fall-back, should Travis ever need it. It has to be clear that I'm not trying to take away his most important defence. It remains an option.

Perhaps because he senses this, he softens. 'The only thing I know about my dad is that apparently I get my temper from him!'

My counsellor antennae are twitching. This is big news! I'm tempted to seize on this very obvious identification between Travis and his father as evidence of the father in his story, of the father presumably invoked at home by his mother whenever Travis's temper flares. Perhaps, over the years, his temper has become an unconscious expression of loyalty to his father, a way of bringing his father back into his mother's house and, at the same time, re-enacting what might have driven them to split up in the first place? Perhaps his father was the original 'mouthy little sod'?

I resist the temptation to pump him for more information. Now isn't the time. We can come back to this. There will be all sorts of other interesting things to know about Travis and, for young people, the need to be interesting is primitive. A baby has to interest its mother and urgently, 'Waaaah!' Unless she recognizes and is interested in her baby, the baby's in trouble: an uninterested mother might abandon her baby. Our need to be interesting never leaves us. Young people will do anything to interest those around them because to be uninteresting is dangerous; it feels like being worthless, like not existing. So if nothing else seems to be working, young people will take all sorts of risks: self-harm, violence, drinking, drugs, getting into trouble – whatever it takes to get someone's attention.

We talk scornfully about children and young people ('only') needing attention as if the rest of us didn't also crave attention. Yet our lives are made up of attention-seeking behaviours. The only difference between young people and adults is that adults have usually found more sophisticated ways of hiding their need. It may no longer be so blatant, but it's just as powerful. The newborn baby screams, 'Waaaah!', thrashing about, desperate to be heard, and years later, young people like Travis come to counselling with a similarly urgent presenting problem, a similar way of getting attention. In effect, they're still screaming 'Waaaah!'; in effect, they're still thrashing about and the more dramatically the better.

As Fonagy *et al.* (2004) make clear, the baby that gets enough regular, attuned attention gradually internalizes a sense of being *intrinsically* interesting. The baby no longer needs to scream and thrash about in order to attract attention to itself because the parental face is always there, mirroring the baby back to itself, carefully reflecting on the baby until, gradually, the baby learns to reflect on itself, having internalized and developed that capacity (Winnicott 1971).

Some babies never get that attuned, attentive mirroring, however. For some, the only attention they get is when they scream angrily. So if anger is the only thing that gets attention, the baby's repertoire of responses remains narrowed. 'I only exist, I only get noticed when I'm angry, so angry is what I'll become. A mouthy little sod! That's who I'll be. That's my story!'

Travis wants to tell me all about his swearing, his fights, his exclusions; all about the people he's threatened; all about himself as an angry person. I have to listen respectfully to this because it's what he knows. It's what he assumes will make him interesting to me. The idea that I might be genuinely interested in all sorts of other things about him will be very strange and, for Travis, will take a lot of getting used to.

We talk about his passing interest in computer games, his friendship with a boy who moved away, the fun of tickling his half-siblings, the go-cart he started building in the shed with Errol, his mother's partner... I'm clearly just as interested in these things as I am in his anger but I'll have to sustain that interest over a period of time for Travis ever to start believing that these parts of his life might really be interesting. I'm also interested in the earlier parts of his life, of course, and from time to time we go there. In our second meeting I ask again about inheriting his anger from his father. I wonder aloud whether it was his anger that might have got his father kicked out of the army.

Travis says he doesn't know, but doesn't raise any objection to my wondering.

I say I wonder if it was his father's anger that caused his parents to split up.

He replies that, knowing his mother, it was probably 50-50.

Again, my counsellor antennae are twitching but, again, it's best to leave it there with this second revelation: the fact that his father may not have been entirely to blame. This is a brand-new strand of the story, a softening of Travis's original claim that his father was the loser, the unmitigated bad guy.

'Don't get me wrong,' Travis adds, perhaps sensing my interest. 'I love my mum. She's always been there for me.'

'I know,' I say. 'All you're saying is that she's not perfect.'

'Exactly!'

'That no one's perfect…'

If young people can learn to think about, to reflect on themselves, they're less likely to enact their feelings and anxieties. They can bear to wait. They can regulate their behaviour: the very thing that Travis struggles to do. Then when things inevitably go wrong, when someone inevitably says something cruel or disrespectful, they're able to respond in a variety of ways rather than simply lash out every time. And their ability to do this comes from being a varied person, an interesting person, a multi-faceted person, a person with a flexible, nuanced, multi-layered story.

With young people whose lives are fragmented, whose sense of self is disorganized and who are sometimes extremely defended as a result, it often helps if I write a very short autobiography for them. I write in the first person, in the language the young person would use. I mention key events and relationships in their lives. I describe the feelings they wouldn't normally tell anyone about. 'People think I'm confident but I don't always feel like that… The things that have happened make me angry but also make me sad… Sometimes my life feels pointless… I worry that I'm mad… I worry that I'm bad…'

Writing in this way allows me to filter interpretations into the story: things most young people wouldn't be able to say for themselves but might recognize as true. Usually, I end with something like, 'If I've let you read this, it's to help you understand more about my life. You may not be able to do anything to help me, but at least you'll know what my life's like and who I really am.' I put the young person's name at the bottom of the page with the date.

The next time we meet, I explain that I've been thinking about the young person during the week and have written this piece. I read it out. Often the young person is moved if I've managed to capture the really important but normally unsaid things. At the end, I ask if I've got it right, if I've understood correctly. If necessary, I make changes on the computer in my room and print off another copy, or I go away and make the changes before we meet again. I give the young person the finished autobiography to take away and to show to whomsoever they wish. Some young people show no one; some say they showed it to a friend or to a teacher. Occasionally, someone comes back the next week and complains, 'I accidentally left it on the kitchen table and my mum read it. God!'

After we've been meeting for several weeks, I decide to do this with Travis as a way of reflecting him back to himself, reflecting back someone much more interesting than just 'a mouthy little sod'. I explain to him what I've done and that I may have misunderstood some bits, but that I'll be interested in what he thinks.

He says nothing, waiting in his chair, unsure how to react.

My name's Travis Lynch. If I'm letting you read this, it's to help you understand about me and about my life. People think they know me but they don't. They just think I'm angry all the time, that I'm always getting into fights and that I don't care.

It's true that I do get angry and I am good at sticking up for myself. I might look like I don't care but I care a lot about some things. I care about things that aren't fair, like bullying and cruelty to animals. I hate it when people mistreat animals who can't defend themselves.

My mum and dad split up when I was two. In some ways this has made me a stronger person, good at sticking up for myself, but in other ways I don't have as much confidence as people think. I get on with my life but I always wonder what it would have been like if my mum and dad had stayed together.

For a long time it was just me and my mum. Then she met Errol and now they've got two children who are my half-sister and brother. I love them to bits, even if they can be annoying at times. But being annoying isn't really their fault. They're just young.

I get on with my mum and I'd die for her. But at the same time she can be a pain when she's nagging me all the time. People think I must be jealous of my half-sister and brother because they get all the attention, but I'm not. The past is the past, but sometimes I can't help wishing that it was just me and my mum again, although I know she's got to have her own life and so have I. I tell her some things about my life but I don't tell her things that would upset her.

I've started thinking about my dad recently. Part of me hates him for leaving us but I know that sometimes it's for the best. Apparently he was angry all the time and I sometimes wonder if he's changed. I wonder if he ever thinks about us. I don't know if I'd want to meet him. His mum still sends me a card at Christmas, so I suppose I could get in touch with her if I wanted. This might sound weird, but it's like I'm interested in him and not interested in him. Sometimes, if I see a man staring at me in the street, I wonder if it's my dad. That might sound stupid, but it's the truth.

I can be a really good friend if people get to know me. I can be really loyal because I know how much it matters when you've got someone to watch your back. And it might sound a bit big-headed, but I know I can be really kind and fun to be with. I like a laugh.

I'm pissed off about a lot of things in my life and sometimes I take that out on other people. Sometimes I get sad but I don't tell anyone. Sometimes when I'm sad I act angry.

If I've let you read this, I hope you understand. I know I can't change the things that have happened in my life but it's good when people understand what I'm really like.

Travis Lynch

I look up slowly. There's a tear in Travis's eye but he quickly manages to make it go away.

'Yeah,' he says. 'Yeah...'

12

The Myth of Anger Management

In supervision sessions with counsellors, we come back again and again to anger. Where's the young person's anger? How's it being expressed? How's it being defended against? Is it being split off? Repressed? Somatized? How can it be understood as a potentially creative force in the young person's life? How can it be verbalized so that it doesn't have to be enacted? Listening and trying to understand young people's anger is hugely important, but much of my own counselling work with young people has been in hard-pressed schools where the institutional longing for a quick fix never goes away, especially where angry young people are concerned...

Ellie's furious, for example. She wants to kill Roz Karlson, who deliberately went off with Donna's boyfriend at the weekend. And Donna is Ellie's best friend. 'So now Donna's in a right state with her heart broken!' says Ellie, seething. 'God, I hate Roz Karlson! And I hate this school! They can kick me out if they want – I don't care!'

I could suggest that she's over-reacting. After all, it wasn't Ellie's own boyfriend who succumbed to Roz and – for God's sake – a bit of ill-advised kissing at a party hardly warrants first-degree murder!

But she's adamant. 'That fucking bitch is dead when I see her!'

Working in schools, like many of my supervisees, I'm often asked to provide 'anger management' for young people who lose their tempers or seem to be in a state of perpetual rage. Everyone's heard of this thing called 'anger management' and everyone seems to think that it'll be great for the young people they know. By the sound of it, it'll sort everything out; it'll make family life happy again; it'll stop young people being excluded from school and turn them into loving, obedient sons and daughters. I'm supposed to be Professor Dumbledore dispensing this magic potion called 'anger management'.

Ellie admits that she's had a bad week. Her dad's been arguing with her mum on the phone about money, and that always puts her in a bad mood, she says. She's also been worrying about her own boyfriend and what he gets up to when she's not there. Plus, she got a detention today for something that wasn't even her fault. 'But I'm still not happy about what that bitch Karlson did! She knew he was going out with Donna!'

A few young people come to see me for the first time and (not quite understanding) say 'I've got anger management!' as if they've got some kind of disease. They may well be feeling angry or their anger may be a convenient defence against much more difficult feelings but, either way, they've been led to believe that being angry means that there's something wrong with them.

I could explain to them something about the physiology of anger. I could suggest breathing exercises or trying to think different thoughts whenever they begin to feel angry. Instead I find myself listening to stories of promises broken, love betrayed, attachments ripped apart and, more often than not, find myself saying, 'I'm not surprised you're angry!'

The young person heaves a sigh of relief.

I'm not denigrating good work done with young people in the name of 'anger management' or any other contemporary potion. If the work's good, it'll be because it allows young people to talk safely about their feelings and not because it provides them with a quick solution. My concern is that we're sometimes inclined to simplify life's most difficult problems: if he's unhappy, give him a pill; if people are complex and time-consuming, pretend they're simple; if she's angry, find a magician to give her a dose of 'anger management' and then she won't be angry any more.

Ellie gets angry because she cares. If she were indifferent to other people and to the things that have happened in her life, she wouldn't bother to be angry. And if she *couldn't* be angry, she'd be depressed. So her anger is healthy. It keeps her alive, passionate, energized, creative. And of course her anger with Roz Karlson and 'this school' is about far more important things…

I learn that her father left when she was five but kept in touch, promising holidays and, when they never happened, promising to spend time at weekends with his daughter. That never happened either. He started a new family and moved further away. Apparently he and his partner have just had a baby girl. Ellie's been hurt by all this and yet, even now, can't give up on the dream of a father who'll love her and be proud of her, who'll be interested in her friends, who'll admire her new clothes, who'll want to watch films with her and be pleased to have her as a daughter.

Wherever she goes, Ellie carries a sense of betrayal with her. It hurts. Despite everything that's happened, she still wants to believe the promises that other people make and break: the promises of a father who said he'd always be there for her, the promises of numerous boyfriends who said they'd always love her, of friends who promised to keep secrets, of professionals who promised to do all kinds of things to help her. When they break their promises, the betrayed feeling kicks in and, rather than feel the hurt, the loneliness, the emptiness, Ellie fills herself up with anger. She knows *exactly* what it's like to be Donna.

Anger can't be managed away. Good work done with angry young people will always involve listening, listening and listening again because young people have reasons to be angry. Usually they're angry because they've been hurt, because painful things have happened in their lives and because those things have been unfair. Anger is often an ethical response to injustice. Nelson Mandela was angry. Jesus Christ was angry. Over the centuries, the world has made progress because people got angry.

Of course, what we *do* with our anger, the *way* we express anger matters hugely. Hitting people, swearing at them, damaging their property or killing Roz Karlson are absolutely not acceptable ways of expressing anger. But anger itself isn't the problem. The problem is when no one's prepared to listen to the anger. When adults won't listen to anger expressed as *words* (usually because the adults are so angry themselves), young people are obliged to turn their words into *actions* in order to be heard or to get some kind of response. Unfortunately, that's when all hell breaks loose and Dumbledore is summoned.

Ellie's anger is out of proportion because what Roz Karlson did with Donna's boyfriend taps into so much of her own experience: not only into her experience of her dad but also into her relationship with Euton, the latest in a long line of boyfriends.

'He's my life!' she says. 'I don't know what I'd do without him. I love him so much!'

For Ellie he's become a kind of 'selfobject': a relationship annexed to keep her safe, to complete her sense of being someone (Kohut 1971). He's good-looking. She can tell him things. He's funny. Losing him would be like losing part of herself; it would be like having a limb cut off. And whenever she's reminded of the possibility of this happening – when he doesn't reply to her texts, when she doesn't know exactly where he is – she screams with fear, with the agony of such an imagined loss. 'I'm going to kill Roz Karlson!' sounds very specific but it's about much more than just some girl who happened to kiss Ellie's best friend's boyfriend.

The danger in a school is that – with or without expletives – Ellie will announce her intention to kill Roz Karlson in front of a teacher who'll feel obliged to say something disapproving. At that, Ellie is likely to launch herself into a gleeful frenzy of screaming and swearing guaranteed to get herself excluded from school. She'll do it because it'll feel so good to stop thinking for those 20 mad seconds in the corridor or classroom as she lets go of all personal responsibility, as she reverts to being a child again, a baby thrashing about, raging mindlessly against life's frustrations, against the very existence of other people (Luxmoore 2006).

At that point, someone in the school hierarchy will have been alerted and will arrive to ask *why* she's behaving this way. Ellie won't be able to answer because, when we're full of feeling, 'why' questions don't work. Right now, she has no idea *why*. Unable to answer, she'll probably just swear some more and get herself into further trouble.

If, at a later date, I were to ask her how old she *feels* when she loses it so spectacularly, I imagine her admitting that she feels about five years old… Exactly the age she was when her father began to break his promises.

There are plenty of young people like Ellie – big, hard, scary incredible hulks – who lose it and then, minutes later, shut away in the privacy of someone's office, find themselves crying and crying because underneath the anger there are so many other feelings waiting to be told, waiting to be heard – sad feelings, hurt feelings, lonely feelings. My work with Ellie will involve hearing these feelings. It'll involve not taking her sweary anger at face value but trying to understand the other, more frightening things that her anger protects her from feeling. We only learn to regulate our feelings (the aim of 'anger management') once they're recognized and understood by other people (Fonagy *et al.* 2004). A baby learns this under the gaze of an attentive parent who recognizes and responds to the baby's feelings. Eventually the baby internalizes this capacity to recognize its feelings and can do the job for itself without needing a parent to be physically present any longer. But for young people who've never experienced that attentive gaze, who haven't yet developed the capacity to recognize and think about their own feelings, there's no alternative to the experience of being well listened to by another person and then slowly, gradually developing an ability to regulate and listen to themselves.

'She *so* pisses me off!' says Ellie. 'Going round like she's something special! She's got nothing to be proud of, the slag!'

I ask what she'd say to Roz if she ever had the opportunity.

'I wouldn't say anything! I'd just kill her!'

'If you could kill her with words…?'

'I don't know… I hate her so much! I'd tell her she's got no right to go round messing up other people's lives.'

'Because people get hurt…'

'Yeah, they do! Like Donna. Her heart's broken – she's been crying all day!'

'And you know what that feels like…'

'Yeah, I do!' She checks herself. 'How d'you know that?'

'Because you said about your dad and what it's like when he messes you around.'

'Yeah! I hate him as well. And his stupid bitch girlfriend!'

'Maybe he's broken your heart a bit?'

She stops in her tracks, suddenly sad. 'Yeah…'

Listening to another person's anger is difficult if we're angry ourselves or scared of our own anger. Through the wonders of projective identification, young people regularly defend against feeling their own anger by giving it to someone else to feel – by winding them up, in effect. It'll be hard for Ellie's mother or for her teachers to listen, to *really* listen, if they themselves are full of anger: anger at Ellie's behaviour ('Why should I bother listening to Ellie? She never listens to anyone else!'); anger at the unfairness of being a parent or teacher never getting it right and never getting any recognition for trying so hard. Unable or unwilling to listen, it's tempting to send for Dumbledore and his magic potion.

'My mum's been wanting me to do anger management for ages,' says Ellie. 'She says if I don't sort myself out then I'm going to have to find somewhere else to live.'

'What do you feel about that?'

'I know I get angry,' she says. 'But I can't help it!'

'Well, maybe your anger's important,' I say. 'Maybe you've got things to be angry about!'

She laughs. 'You can say that again!'

'And maybe it keeps you safe sometimes. Maybe it scares people off and then there's no danger of them finding out what you really feel!'

She thinks about this.

There are some young people for whom the anger button appears always to be 'on', hiding more vulnerable feelings. For other young people, anger can be an achievement: better than self-harming or starving and more honest than winding people up. There are girls, for example, who find themselves crying when they're not sad at all: in fact, they're angry but somehow the anger always gets turned into tears.

Ellie's different. 'To be honest,' she says, 'I've been pissed off for really a long time. For longer than today... I've been pissed off all my life!'

13

Working with Anger

Looking agitated, Rachel sits down and begins to tell me about a 13-year-old boy. 'Apparently he gets angry all the time, but he says he actually enjoys being angry! He doesn't feel sorry at all. He told me he likes fighting and *enjoys* inflicting pain on people…'

When counsellors start work in schools, they're tested by individual students and by the institution to see if they'll panic, to see how robust they are, to see if they've got a magic wand (Luxmoore 2014). Rachel is the new counsellor in her school. She looks at me as if she's expecting me to rescue her from this particular boy, or at least to tell her what to do. I wonder to myself whether the school effectively wants Rachel to rescue it from all its angry boys? 'We've got this boy, Rachel. He's impossible. You're new. It's your job to transform him, okay?'

Under pressure, counsellors in schools mustn't panic, mustn't give up and mustn't be tempted into prescribing cheap behavioural solutions, most of which will almost certainly fail within a fortnight. Nor must they take the presenting issue at face value. The school will always be hoping for a panacea, and the pressure on the counsellor to perform behavioural miracles will always be great. But the presenting issue – in this case, anger – will almost certainly be symptomatic of a wider issue for the school (Luxmoore 2014).

Rachel tells me about the boy's family, and by the sound of it, he has a thousand reasons to be angry. His father left before he can remember but is remembered in the family as 'evil' and 'violent'.

His mother has boyfriends who come and go. He has younger half-siblings. And he's 13! He sounds like a boy trying to work out who he's supposed to be, but with no father for comparison, only a father's reputation. And then, thrown into the 13-year-old mix are peer relationships, academic pressures, worrying about the future, sexuality… It sounds as if Rachel's boy is well and truly stuck.

We talk about anger as healthy ('Young people get angry because they care'), about anger as a defence (Luxmoore 2006) and as a way of feeling alive. I confess to Rachel that I'm always pleased when young people are angry because it means that they're alive. I remind her that young people often enact their anger when no one's prepared to listen to it expressed as words. She and I talk about anger as regressive; about the delights of 'losing it', of returning temporarily to a baby-state, screaming and thrashing around (Luxmoore 2006). We talk about anger as an ethical response to injustice and about people sometimes expressing anger on behalf of other people.

Rachel's writing some of these things down but doesn't look convinced. 'I get all that,' she says, 'but he's angry the *whole time*, and says he enjoys it! So I was wondering if, really, he should be seeing someone from outside school? In case there's something wrong with him…' She looks at me doubtfully. 'What do you think?'

She's a conscientious counsellor who wants the best for the young people she's seeing. Like any counsellor, she worries about any of them developing a mental illness, especially one that might have been prevented.

I ask her what she was like when she was 13.

'Not really very angry,' she says. 'Well, I did get angry sometimes with my brothers and with my sister but only normal brother–sister stuff. Normal anger…'

She has two teenage children of her own. 'How are your kids with anger?'

'Pretty good!' she says. 'Sometimes I think it's what they do best!'

We could say more, but Rachel sounds comfortable enough with her own anger and with her children's anger. No particular connections to be made there. I'm about to return to the angry boy in school…

'My husband can be pretty angry, though.' The warmth has gone from her voice. 'When he doesn't like something the kids have done. Or something he thinks I've done wrong…'

I ask her to say a little more.

'I don't know if it's relevant to supervision,' she answers, defensively. 'I mean, what do you want to know?'

'Whatever you want to tell me, Rachel. But don't if you think it's not relevant. It would only be relevant if it affects or informs your work with young people in some way.'

She says nothing, thinking about this. I wonder whether to change the subject.

'Well, if you really want to know,' she says, looking away, 'we're thinking of separating. We've been thinking about it for a while. He's away for most of the week and every time he's back it feels like a dark cloud descending on the house.'

Her face tightens as if she's about to cry. I ask Rachel if she wants to separate from her husband.

She checks herself as the feelings well up inside and, swallowing, she lets the moment pass. 'I just think it would probably be better for everyone. For the kids, but also for me because I don't know how much more of it I can stand. He's always in a bad mood, always complaining about something, and always taking it out on someone – usually me. And if it's not me, then he's shouting and throwing things around in his study. And this has been going on for years. The kids get scared. I get scared. None of us are happy.' She glances across. 'Sorry, you didn't really want to hear this!'

I remind her that I'm still listening.

'I don't think there's much more to say, really. That's just the way it is at the moment. Pretty shit!'

I find myself wondering about her angry boy at school – another angry person in her life whose behaviour never seems to change. 'So you go from an angry man at home, Rachel, to an angry boy at school, and then back to an angry man at home… It would make sense that you might want someone else to look after the angry boy at school.'

She's thoughtful. 'D'you think that's what I'm doing? Passing the buck?'

'Well, it would make sense that if you're living with anger at home, you certainly wouldn't want to be working with it all the time in school!'

'Not all the kids in school are angry,' she smiles. 'It's only this particular boy that I'm worried about. But you're right. It would make sense.'

She's wise enough to go away and think about this by herself, so I don't press the point. 'It doesn't sound as if there's anything fundamentally wrong with your boy,' I say. 'It sounds as if he's got plenty of good reasons to be angry, and you might have your own good reasons for shying away from his anger at the moment. But I suppose the task is to help him learn to think about himself rather than just act out his anger at his own or at other people's expense…'

So many young people come to counselling full of feelings that they can't think about or regulate because they don't know how to do that, because no one has ever sat with them and helped them reflect on themselves. Once young people have developed what Fonagy *et al.* (2004) call 'reflective-self function' (as I described in the last chapter), they can better regulate their behaviour. They no longer need to run around being angry all the time.

Oddly, schools aren't always very good at reflecting on things. Teachers are expected to do, do, do. To stop and reflect is to risk being accused of time-wasting, and it's easy for counsellors in schools to get caught up in this, trying to prove their own usefulness through doing, doing, doing, dashing around, impossibly busy, exuding stress. Yet all this doing is often defensive. Like the angry action of Rachel's boy, it stops us from having to think, from having to take responsibility for ourselves, from considering our effect on others.

There's no panacea. Rachel's job is to sit with the boy and help him to reflect, to think about all that's fuelling his anger, all that's happened in his life, all the fair and unfair things. It'll be slow work. No magic wand. As Winnicott (1989a) describes, children develop in relation to their environment and 'there is no description of an infant that leaves out the behaviour of the person caring for the infant' (p.445). Rachel will play her part in his development and so will other people in the boy's life. For her, there'll be the additional task of helping the school bear its own anger: anger in the staffroom when the job seems impossible; anger in the corridors when other people are frustrating; anger in the headteacher's office when the world makes life more difficult than it needs to be; anger the school struggles to bear and gives to Rachel to resolve: Rachel The Magician, Rachel The Rescuer.

We talk about how she might do this by becoming a presence in the staffroom, listening to staff, running training for staff, developing a relationship with the headteacher, looking for opportunities to share her experience with her school colleagues.

'Until the whole school calms down and becomes more confident with anger, especially staffroom anger, they'll always be sending you impossibly angry young people, Rachel.'

She looks happier. 'So you don't think there's anything necessarily wrong with my boy?'

I say that I doubt it. 'I'm not saying that no young people ever get ill. It's just that in schools it's easy for people to panic, imagining any difficult behaviour to be a sign of mental illness, and then they get their panic into the person they imagine might be able to help. In this case, you! You have to withstand that, bear their panic, stay calm and stay true to what you know, which is that anger is potentially healthy, is sometimes defensive, and that change is usually slow.'

'And I have to be aware of not taking stuff from home into school!'

'You can't help that. None of us can. But you have to be aware of it, yes.'

She begins to gather up her notes.

I say that I hope things at home will improve in one way or another.

She winces, trying to smile, suddenly looking very alone.

14

The Waiting List

Marvin complains that members of staff at his school are forever panicking. They panic if someone dies or is dying. They panic about sex, about self-harm and about anyone who mentions the word 'suicide'. At the first sign of trouble, they send their students off to see Marvin, the counsellor. 'He'll be able to help you!' they say. 'He's more qualified to help, especially when it comes to this sort of thing. And he's got more time...'

Overrun with young people, Marvin's fed up. He wishes his colleagues would sort it out themselves. He tells me that he tried to talk to the headteacher about the problem but their meeting was ended when Carol, the head's PA, burst in, saying, 'I've just had a phone call asking if Marvin can come to the medical room as quickly as possible because there's a student punching a wall and refusing to talk to anyone!'

Marvin pointed out to the headteacher that this was another example of exactly what he was talking about: the school's over-reliance on him for psychological support.

'I know,' said the head. 'Clearly we've got an issue here. But if you could go and see the student that would be great and I'll get Carol to re-schedule our meeting for another time when – hopefully – we'll be able to continue this conversation without interruptions...'

Marvin's experience isn't unusual. There may be an adolescent mental health crisis but it's not necessarily a crisis of increased mental illness. The developmental tasks of adolescence haven't suddenly changed. The Association for Young People's Health (2015), an organization gathering together all the available research, reports that, in the UK, there's no clear evidence to suggest that adolescent mental illness has increased. Certain *behaviours* have undoubtedly increased: there's more self-harming and there are more young people with eating disorders. There are also many more young people complaining of 'anxiety' and 'depression' but adolescent suicides, unplanned pregnancies, physical fighting and drug and alcohol abuse among young people have all decreased.

If there's a crisis, it may – in part – be a crisis of confidence in the ability of ordinary people, people like Marvin's colleagues, to support young people going through difficult times.

There are various reasons for this. Adolescence has never happened to an adolescent before. Young people google their symptoms and readily conclude that they must be suffering from 'anxiety' or 'depression', from 'a personality disorder' or, if they're wondering about the apparent pointlessness of life, that they must be suicidal.

Their parents are worried too. Things have changed. Their children have become moody, erratic and hard to read. The world says that successful parenting produces happy children doing productive things. So when they're unhappy and doing bad things, it's hard to work out what might have gone wrong. Parents panic. Young people panic. Parents take their sons and daughters to the doctor, 'just to be on the safe side' and doctors, uncertain about how to interpret the symptoms, refer young people on to mental health agencies, 'just to be on the safe side'.

There's a tendency to pathologize adolescence rather than understand misery and misfortune as some of the many developmental challenges of adolescence. As Alexander (2012) writes, '… what might look like pathology in an adult is actually normal in an adolescent… The adolescent who doesn't allow himself to take a look at the edge is more at risk psychologically than the adolescent who does' (p.172).

Despite this, the DSM, the bible of psychiatry, gets bigger with every edition, pathologizing more and more of what was once thought of as normal life (Davies 2013). This suits insurance and pharmaceutical companies because, with more varieties of mental illness than ever before, there are more opportunities to make money. Yet our understanding of mental illness is, at best, inexact. 'Is she depressed? Is he a suicide risk?' With varying degrees of expertise, mental health professionals muddle through like the rest of us, watching their backs and making their risk assessments based largely on common sense, hoping that young people are telling them the truth. Inevitably, they try to create streamlined services that avoid mess, and when young people insist on being messy, new bureaucracies, new professional protocols are created in an attempt to tidy up the mess. The danger is that people without a professional qualification in listening come to believe that they've got nothing to offer. 'I'm not a qualified counsellor!' says the teacher with *years* of experience. 'Parents aren't always the best listeners,' says the parent who happens to be a very good listener.

It's true that teachers and parents aren't always good listeners and that their role sometimes compromises their listening (most young people need to talk *about* their parents), but the majority of them are good enough, and many young people would rather confide in them than in a here-today-gone-tomorrow stranger, however many qualifications the stranger happens to have. Talking with a stranger can be liberating, but it's the quality of the attachment to the other person that encourages and makes the difference for young people.

Counsellors like Marvin have to assure ordinary adults that they *do* have the skills to make a difference, that most young people would rather talk to someone they know already, that listening and trying to understand is what professional counsellors and psychotherapists are trying to do. *Really* listening and *really* trying to understand. Not dispensing cheap advice.

In Marvin's school, a student killed himself a couple of years ago, so it's understandable that there's collective anxiety about the possibility of something like that ever happening again. 'What could we have done differently? How can we ensure that this never happens again?' Most schools and most universities share the same anxiety. Long risk assessments are carried out in the hope that this will minimize the possibility of anyone killing themselves and, of course, there's always a need for sensible measures to protect young people. But these measures rarely assuage the collective anxiety because everyone knows (but no one wants to admit) that, actually, a young person could kill himself at any time. No one wants to feel responsible for that, so they set other people up to carry their anxiety for them: in this case, Marvin, the person to whom his colleagues turn, convinced that their own efforts would never be enough and happy to believe that Marvin will know exactly what to do.

'I'm getting completely mixed messages from the head,' he says. 'He'll agree with me that other people in school need to take more responsibility, but then he'll go along with a stunt like Carol's. He could have told her to find someone else to help the boy!'

'Or else you could have told Carol?'

'Easy to say, hard to do,' says Marvin, 'especially when I'm getting no back-up from the head...'

'Perhaps you're a victim of your own success,' I suggest. 'You're good, so everyone wants a piece of you.'

'Maybe, but it's not that simple,' he says. 'Most of them just want to believe that there's someone in school who'll make everything all right. I could be the worst counsellor in the world, they'd still be sending people to me!'

Encouraging other professionals to take more responsibility is always difficult. They'll always claim to be too busy, quick to find practical reasons why they can't make themselves available. But underneath their protestations, there's always a lack of confidence. 'I wouldn't know what to say... I'd be afraid of saying the wrong thing...

I've got my own worries, you know… I'm no expert… These things are best left to the professionals…'

'But you *are* a professional!'

'Yes, but I'm not a professional *counsellor*. You're the one with the training and the experience!'

I'm all for counsellors seeing lots of young people. But Marvin also has to learn to say no to staff making their always-urgent referrals and – more painfully – to students approaching him themselves when his diary is already full to overflowing.

He looks annoyed when I mention this. 'I know, I know! You're right. Of course you are…'

'But?'

'But nothing! You're right!'

'So what stops you?' I ask. 'What stops you explaining that your diary is full and that you can't start seeing any new people at the moment? It's the truth, after all…'

'I know,' he says. 'I just hate having to turn people away. Especially when they've made the effort to ask and when I can see how desperate they are.'

He's in a classic bind: wanting to help vulnerable people but then resenting them for being vulnerable. I assure him that turning people away *is* hateful but that there's no alternative. 'Most people will find other ways of getting support,' I say. 'Young people are pretty resourceful. Most of them will muddle through. And your colleagues will be obliged to take more responsibility. But as long as you keep tantalizing them with the possibility that you might just have the magic wand they're searching for, they'll keep sending you whoever happens to be shouting loudest. And you can't work like that. That way, everyone will claim to be suicidal if it's the only way of getting to see you.'

Counsellors are often badly paid and badly resourced. It's tempting for them to lay claim to skills no one else has in making a case for the uniqueness of their contribution. It takes confidence to admit that they're human beings simply trying to understand other human beings. Yet that can be oddly reassuring for other people. 'I've known people who genuinely think I go round reading their minds,' I tell Marvin. 'And when I've assured them that I don't and can't, I think they've been disappointed but also relieved. They've been much more relaxed with me after that... As a counsellor, you have to keep giving the power back to other people, assuring them that they really can do it themselves.'

'Fine,' says Marvin, making a face, 'but the waiting list gets longer and longer!'

'There'll always be a waiting list,' I tell him. 'If you're seeing 50 people, there'll be a waiting list. If you're seeing a hundred, there'll be a waiting list. Word will spread. You can recruit more counsellors but you'll *still* have a waiting list. You have to live with the pressure of that and keep giving the expertise back to your colleagues. Run training for them. Write things for them, explaining what you're learning from your work with young people. Ask them what they're learning. Get them to share their learning with each other. Help them to understand young people better. Offer them supervision... And say no when you're full. Model for them something about the importance of boundaries, about having to bear the panic, about no one having all the answers.'

He smiles for the first time. 'So you're giving me permission?'

'I am, if that's what you need. You can blame me, Marvin!'

'Great,' he says, still smiling, 'I will!'

15

Boundaries

'I've done a bad thing,' says Kerry, 'but I didn't know what else to do...'

As usual, I find myself admiring her honesty. Most of us are cautious about admitting our mistakes, even in supervision where we're supposed to be able to tell anything. But Kerry is never too proud to be wrong. She makes mistakes, talks about them and, as a result, learns very quickly.

'There's a teacher at work and we've been chatting a lot in the staffroom and I really like her. Anyway, I couldn't see any harm in it, so I went for a drink with her, and she was talking all about her life and I was telling her some stuff about my dad and also about Judith...'

Judith is Kerry's partner.

'We had a nice time talking. But now she's asked if she can come and see me for counselling and I don't know what to say.'

'What have you said?'

'Nothing yet. She emailed yesterday and I haven't replied yet.'

Counselling in a school is a job that suits some people and not others. It's never a lonely job because there are always people around, but it's a lonesome job. The counsellor sees lots of young people and sometimes staff as well, but in a sense, the school itself is also the client. The counsellor is always listening for the institutional anxieties and trying to affect them on behalf of everyone, including all those people who will never come for counselling but who matter just as much as those who do (Luxmoore 2014). Everyone in the school is a potential client, therefore, checking out the counsellor from the moment that she walks through the gates, or, in Kerry's case, from a first conversation in the staffroom to a drink in a bar. She's always The Counsellor. So Kerry can't afford to stay hidden away in her room – she has to be out and about, talking to people – but can't afford to be seen to take sides, to sit with one particular group in the staffroom or to become friends with one particular person for fear of compromising her perceived impartiality, her availability as a resource for everyone. Of course counsellors are *friendly* and their friendliness will be reciprocated. But they're always making judgments about how much of themselves to disclose. To disclose nothing would be weird, so counsellors have to answer questions and tell people things about themselves, but always for strategic reasons, to normalize counselling, to demystify themselves. They'll joke, they'll join in, but unlike other members of staff, they'll never have a colleague they can confide in. When they're frustrated or despairing, they can't expect to be contained by colleagues at school because it's the counsellor's job to do the containing.

Happily, there are paybacks. Left largely to their own devices and trusted to get on with it, most counsellors aren't subject to the bureaucratic scrutiny suffered by teachers. Counsellors aren't inspected. They have the satisfaction of contributing to a culture rather than just to a set of exam results. They have the chance to affect the institution in all sorts of subtly creative ways.

But it's a lonesome existence and it's easy to blame the school for this: 'People don't care about my work! The leadership team doesn't understand counselling!' Lonesome is the price Kerry must pay for the privilege of being allowed to close her door and get on with it. Lonesome is the price she must pay for the wonderfully creative opportunities that the job affords.

I say all this to her. 'So don't work as the counsellor in a school, Kerry, if you're not prepared to pay the price.'

She looks deflated.

'Does that sound harsh?'

'No,' she says, 'it's what I thought you'd say. I know I've messed up. But what can I say to Myra? I know that asking for counselling will have been a big deal for her...'

Counsellors are always aware of boundaries and must adapt appropriately to so many different situations. Working with young people and working in a school, counsellors have to be *more* (not less) aware of boundaries, but that doesn't mean that they have to be more draconian. It means becoming more sophisticated in the way they manage boundaries. The best counsellors are always thoughtful about boundaries, always aware of what they're doing, always aware of the consequences, always aware of their own motivations.

So going for a drink and sharing important information about her own life with a potentially needy colleague may not have been Kerry's smartest decision. But she has to live with it. Members of staff at her school know that she's available for them as much as for the students. So she can now reply to Myra saying that, through no fault of Myra's but because of their social relationship, she's unavailable as a counsellor, but unavailable *only* to Myra, not to any other member of staff. Or Kerry can make the best of a bad job and see Myra, retrospectively and gently establishing an appropriate distance between the two of them.

'It's not the end of the world,' I assure her. 'Myra knows that you're a human being, that you struggle with your dad and that you've got a partner. So what? You'll just have to avoid sharing any more of that kind of information with her and, whatever you do, *don't* go for any more drinks!'

Boundaries are guidelines; rarely are they absolute rules. But managing boundaries with young people and in schools requires the confidence to be flexible. There are all sorts of dilemmas to be negotiated where the answer is seldom straightforward...

I'm already seeing the sister and now they want me to start seeing the brother as well... What should I do?

His tutor's asking how the Imran's been getting on in our counselling sessions… What should I say?

Her mother emailed to ask if she can come and see me for herself… What do you think?

The headteacher's son wants a counselling appointment… Should I see him?

My son's starting at the school where I work… Is that okay?

These may be some of the more obvious dilemmas, but counsellors also have to make incidental decisions about boundaries throughout the day: decisions about how to dress, decorate the room, greet people, reply to the questions like 'Did you go anywhere nice for your holiday?' It's rarely simple. I think there's a danger of unconfident counsellors hiding behind black-and-white boundaries for fear of getting it wrong and sometimes in order *not* to have relationships with especially vulnerable young people who are desperate to attach or who are completely chaotic or furious. There's a danger of counsellors keeping the most demanding or scary young people at arm's length in the name of boundaries.

I remember a time when my car wouldn't start. My 15-year-old, long-term, I-hate-school client was passing. He asked what was the matter, looked under the bonnet, tweaked something, and the car started.

It was our most therapeutic moment, allowing him to demonstrate his competence in response to my incompetence. It allowed him to make it up to me for some of the hard times he'd given me in counselling and, in so doing, I think it allowed him – at an unconscious, transferential level – to practise a less antagonistic, more collaborative relationship with a father-figure. Had I avoided speaking to him because we were no longer in the counselling room, had I declined his offer of help because it might have led to a confusion of roles, none of this would have been possible. And, in any case, these responses would have been weird. Counsellors working with young people have to normalize the processes of counselling (Luxmoore 2014) and that involves normalizing themselves, as I argued in Chapter 6.

'It's tricky,' I say to Kerry. 'It's tricky judging how ready a person might be for a more relaxed kind of relationship.'

We're meeting in my living room. She sits facing my books, a photograph of my father and an array of birthday cards on the mantelpiece.

'You and I could sit in a bare room, for example. That way, I'd be giving away very little about myself, and maybe with some of my supervisees that would be appropriate. But it's always a boundary decision. With you I'm judging that you can cope with knowing quite a lot about me, Kerry. I'm judging that it won't interfere with our work together, and that in terms of your professional development, you're ready to know certain things about me.'

'But maybe I'm not ready,' she laughs, 'if I'm messing things up, like with Myra! Maybe you should be putting me in some bare lockup room until I've learned my lesson!'

Young people are always noticing the way their counsellors work with boundaries: the times when their counsellors won't budge and the times when they make compromises. They're always interested in their counsellor's reasoning, because learning to manage boundaries is a huge part of any young person's development. Boundaries might be relatively straightforward for a child ('Do this! Don't do that!'), but with young people they stop being straightforward. Young people must begin to live with the mysteries of 'appropriateness', of one person's truth not being the same as another person's, of friendship being relative. They're learning that secrecy and privacy aren't the same thing (Luxmoore 2016), that there are degrees of privacy (Luxmoore 2000). Counsellors modelling a black-and-white approach to everything don't do young people any favours.

'Any lessons I've learned', I say to Kerry, 'are because I've made mistakes. When I was a teacher, I had to get used to having informal relationships with students in the corridor and then, five minutes later, having more formal relationships with them in the classroom, giving a homework detention to the same boy I'd just been chatting with about football. As a youth worker, I had to confiscate vodka from the same girl who, earlier in the evening, had been enthusiastically helping me to set up the concert. In one job, I was simultaneously the youth worker and the school counsellor where, because of his bad behaviour, I had to ban from the youth centre the same boy who was seeing me for counselling in school. I'd be making boundary judgments with every interaction. Believe me, I've got close to plenty of Myras and then wished I hadn't. But we learn. We get better at the job. Parents and other authority-figures have exactly the same dilemmas. It's never about being slack on boundaries. It's about being skillful with boundaries… So what about Myra?'

'I'll see her,' Kerry says, 'for the reasons you said.'

'And if she asks to go for another drink?'

'I'll say that I enjoyed our drink, but that in order to help her, I'm going to concentrate on our counselling relationship where she can have the time without having to share it with me.'

'And if she says, "No, it's fine, I like hearing about your life, Kerry!"'

'Then I'll say… Er, what will I say?' She pauses, thinking. 'I'll say that it's kind of her to think of me, but that in order to help her properly in counselling, it's better if we don't blur the two relationships, but save any social relationship maybe for the future. I'll say that she has other people to go for a drink with, but only one counsellor to see for counselling!'

'Very good! And what if she says that she *hasn't* actually got anyone else to go for a drink with?'

'Then I'll say that I'm looking forward to hearing about that in counselling… Oh hell!'

We both laugh.

'It'll be fine, Kerry. It might be a bit of a muddle at first, but it'll be fine.'

She takes a deep breath. 'I bloody hope so!'

16

Self-Disclosure

I remember a friend telling me about going to see a very austere therapist who never said anything about herself as she listened impassively throughout the two years of their relationship. 'The best thing about the whole therapy', said my friend, 'was one time when I got there on a really hot summer's day, and she could see I was desperate for a drink of water, and she actually got me one. It was the only time she did anything like that, and to be honest, it was the thing that meant the most to me. That one thing! I've never forgotten!'

Research suggests that it's never a particular theoretical model or single interpretation that makes the therapeutic difference: it's the quality of the relationship between the two human beings in the room (Yalom 1980): the one cast as helper and the other cast as person needing help. There are plenty of people who tell therapy stories like my friend's: stories not about moments of piercing intellectual insight, but about simple moments of human contact.

Young people are curious about the person sitting with them. 'Are you married?' they ask their counsellors. 'D'you have kids? Did you get on with your parents? Have you ever had counselling yourself?'

In the name of 'boundaries', many counsellors are taught to say nothing about themselves, but there's no such thing as a blank screen. We can pretend otherwise, but – as I said in the last chapter – the way we dress, speak, style our hair and decorate our room allows young people to infer a lot about us. Counsellors are always inadvertently revealing things about themselves. Of course, a proper attention to boundaries is part of what makes any relationship feel safe. Without boundaries, we're lost. It's just that there are enabling boundaries and disabling boundaries. Some boundaried relationships free us to develop as people, while others are claustrophobic, stilted, drained of life by the constraints we impose in the name of boundaries...

'Are you married?'

'Why are you asking?'

'Well, d'you have any kids?'

'I can't tell you that.'

'Why not? I'm only asking! Did you get on with your parents when you were young?'

'That's my business.'

'Okay, so have you had counselling yourself?'

'I thought we were here to discuss you, not me!'

Counsellors working with young people have to be *more* aware of boundaries than counsellors working with adults. Adults will, on the whole, be less overtly inquisitive and more accepting of the presumed 'rules' of counselling whereby a counsellor will expect to say very little about herself. But young people are different. They need and rely on boundaries, but they also challenge boundaries. They're perplexed by the idea of one rule for all because on the one hand it's fair – everyone gets the same treatment; but on the other hand it's impersonal – it fails to recognize individual needs. Young or old, we want a personal relationship with our counsellor, as with a teacher or a doctor. Had my friend found out that, in fact, his therapist regularly gave glasses of water to everyone, I imagine he'd have felt very differently! It was the fact that she was prepared to make a special allowance on a hot day that meant something. 'It was as if, for once, she actually cared about me,' he said.

Most adults come to therapy with a rough idea of what to expect. They know that it's likely to feel a bit weird and that their therapist might seem a bit po-faced. Yet despite this, they sign up and are prepared to go along to the session and see what happens. But there are adults who don't go along; in fact, there are some adults who wouldn't be seen dead going to talk with a stranger about whom they know nothing and where the conversation is distinctly one-sided. These adults might be desperate for help but would rather stick with the devil they know than risk another new and potentially unsettling experience. Young people are the same, except that they have even *less* experience of strange situations and even *less* confidence in dealing with strangers.

Because of this, counsellors working with young people have to become especially skilled at adapting to each person, at remaining flexible, at normalizing the situation where 'normal' involves some kind of exchange. They need a wide repertoire of therapeutic responses, and part of that repertoire will be the extent to which – for carefully thought-out reasons – they do or don't say anything about themselves to the young person sitting opposite.

From the moment that a young person walks into the counselling room, the counsellor is deciding what kind of relationship this young person needs and is ready for. How to greet the young person? How to break the ice? How spontaneous to be? Does the counsellor mention the weather, her terrible journey, the drilling noise outside the window or the fact that she's got a cold and is likely to be coughing a lot? How does the counsellor respond when a young person is late or doesn't turn up? How firm, how irritated, how accepting should she be? Lateness is often a kind of reality test, a way of testing the counsellor's personal boundaries. 'Will she be endlessly accepting of my lateness or will she get real with me? If she's feeling pissed off with me for being late, will she say so?'

Most of us regress when we start counselling. In an unfamiliar setting, we hope that our counsellor will know what to do and will call the shots, making it easier for us to participate. Before long, we'll probably be ready to move on, feeling more confident in asserting and taking responsibility for ourselves. But each of us is different; we develop at different speeds. We hope that our counsellor will anticipate our readiness to move on so that we don't stagnate, but at the same time we don't want to be moved on before we're ready.

So at what point are we ready for the idea that our counsellor might actually be a quirky, flawed human being who goes to the toilet like the rest of us? At what point are we ready to engage with our counsellor's 'ordinariness' (Luxmoore 2011), with the extent to which our counsellor is like us in some ways and unlike us in others? A baby takes a long time to distinguish itself from its parent. Coming to terms with its own separateness and with its parent's fallibility might take a lifetime. Young people effectively begin their relationship with a counsellor in a baby-state and then slowly grow up, separating and growing away from the counsellor. The counsellor's use of self-disclosure can help and hinder that process.

Fifteen-year-old Flora, for example, is talking to me in counselling about her grandfather. He's dying and she says that she feels uncomfortable whenever she thinks about him. Apparently everyone in the family is trying to be happy, and her mum talks of 'keeping things as normal as possible', so Flora's trying to keep things as normal as possible, but it feels to her as if everyone in the family is pretending that somehow her grandfather *isn't* really dying.

She's a kind, well-behaved girl who's come to see me because of the 'anxiety' she attributes to her approaching exams. The fact that her grandfather happens to be dying has only emerged as we've talked about her life after the exams. 'I'm worried that I'll mess everything up,' she says, still talking about the exams, 'and that I'll end up letting everyone down.'

I wonder to myself whether she's talking obliquely about her grandfather's death and about whether she'll be able to keep up the family pretence that everything is normal, worrying all the while that she's letting everyone down. I wonder how much her talk of 'anxiety' alludes to the very mixed feelings she has about her grandfather dying.

At the same time as Flora and I are meeting, my father happens to be dying of old age, having been in a nursing home for a long time, deteriorating slowly. I have a hunch and want to share something of this story with Flora, but wonder to myself whether this is merely for my own satisfaction or because I genuinely think that it might help her. Am I on the verge of saying something about my father for her sake or mine?

I decide to risk it. I tell her that my father is dying of old age, perfectly normally, but that when I'm with him I'm torn between the part of me that wants him to recover and the part of me that wants him to hurry up and die. I tell her that I think my feelings are normal but that sometimes I feel a bit guilty about the part of me that wishes he'd hurry up and die.

I tell her this, not making any overt connection with Flora's own story. I don't ask her to relate to mine. I don't say, 'Do you sometimes feel like that, Flora?' I simply state the facts, but my hunch is that part of Flora *does* wish that her grandfather would hurry up and die, and my hunch comes from never having met the relative of a dying person for whom this sentiment wasn't partly true. But it's a sentiment always disavowed as shameful and unworthy of kind, well-behaved people who love their dying relatives.

'I feel a bit like that sometimes,' says Flora, unprompted.

I say that I'm not surprised. She smiles, looking relieved, and we go on to talk about something else.

It was a high-risk strategy, but my intention was to give kind, well-behaved Flora permission to feel a mixture of feelings and, on balance, I think that I probably succeeded in doing this. Merely telling her that my father was dying would have served no useful purpose, especially as fathers outrank grandfathers in the popular bereavement stakes. Flora might well have felt that her own experience with a grandfather was necessarily less important than mine with a father. And had it been the case, and had I told her that my father was dying a particularly horrible death, that would have crushed her experience altogether.

'Who am I to complain about my grandfather,' she might have thought, 'when his father's dying such a terrible death! Poor Nick!'

If 'anxiety' is a word that sometimes describes mixed feelings (Luxmoore 2016) – loving as well as hating, wanting a person to live *and* die – then naming those feelings takes away some of their power to shame and disturb us. Of course, telling a young person about my dying father is a much more portentous piece of self-disclosure than a therapist fetching her client a glass of water, but the issue is the same: 'Why am I doing this? Who's it really for and will it help or hinder the therapeutic task?'

Sometimes a carefully chosen moment of therapist self-disclosure serves to humanize, to detoxify a young person's experience without the banality of a therapist saying, 'Lots of people go through what you're going through ...' Sometimes self-disclosure sets an emotional tone, modelling for young people a containing of experience. I think I probably modelled that for Flora, telling my story in a way that I hope was neither heartless nor hysterical.

When a young person's formative experiences have been characterized by parental withholding, when a parent has never disclosed anything about themselves to a son or daughter, the therapist potentially becomes what Hurry (1998) calls a 'developmental object', offering a different, reparative experience: a rare but developmentally important experience of mutuality. In some humanistic therapeutic modalities, self-disclosure is the norm. The last part of a psychodrama psychotherapy session, for example, is a chance for the other participants in the group – *including* the therapist – to share their own points of identification with the person whose issue has just been explored in the group. Typically, group members will share something from their own lives with which the issue has resonated. This isn't an opportunity for anyone to give anyone else advice. The therapist shares like any other member of the group while remaining responsible for the overall containment and safety of the group. Managed well, this sharing process becomes part of what contains the group so that members leave the session feeling connected and safe. Whatever the therapist shares from her own life is truthful and sincere, but is also what she thinks the group can tolerate. On a particular occasion, she might be feeling especially vulnerable and affected by the group's work but might judge that the extent of her personal vulnerability isn't appropriate to share with the group at that precise moment.

The same principle applies to counselling with young people. Psychodramatists would describe the group's sharing as a way of 're-clothing' the person who's been exploring an issue, so that he or she doesn't leave the session feeling emotionally naked. Connecting with other people through their stories allows an equilibrium to be restored. The therapist will deliberately moderate the tone of the group's sharing: probing the person who sounds glib, curtailing the person whose story threatens to go on for ever and intervening with the person whose words threaten to undo whatever good work the group has just done. In these ways, the therapist is always making clinical judgments about what's in the best interests of the group, just as the counsellor is always making judgments about what kind of self-disclosure – if any – is in the best interests of a young person.

Winnicott's proposal in 'The Use of an Object' (1989b) is that we move from object-relating to object-usage, from seeing the therapist as an extension of ourselves, to seeing the therapist as a figure in her own right to be appreciated or 'used' for who she is. One of the enduring tasks of therapy with young people is helping them to exist as separate, individuated people in the world, enjoying relationships with other people while remaining ultimately responsible for themselves (Glasser 1979). In roundabout ways, young people are always asking, 'In the light of all that's happened in my life so far, to what extent am I now responsible for myself? Are other people still going to take responsibility for me? Where do I begin and other people end?' A counsellor's self-disclosure will always say something to a young person about whether she's like or unlike her counsellor:

identified and merged with the counsellor or autonomous and separate, a different person.

Any counsellor's self-disclosure relies, therefore, on the young person being ready to see the counsellor as a separate person rather than just a transferential projection, a narcissistic extension of the young person. This means that self-disclosure is sometimes more appropriate towards the end of a therapeutic relationship when the young person is developmentally ready to take the counsellor off her pedestal. Of course, once we become aware of our counsellor as a 'real' person, she is (for the time being) diminished in our eyes so that, initially, we're inclined to be dismissive, full of disdain towards the poor counsellor in the same way that we feel disdainful towards our parents once we realize that – shock! horror! – they get things wrong sometimes and don't know everything. In time, we come to realize that, for all their limitations, our parents are still useful, interesting, worthwhile people. The same applies to counsellors.

Counsellors will be less likely to allow this developmental process to happen, though, if they feel *personally* diminished by a young person's disillusionment and scorn. 'I thought you knew everything! I thought you had your life all worked out. But now it turns out that you're no better than me!' Never disclosing anything about oneself can sometimes be a way of maintaining the illusion of therapeutic omniscience. It may protect the therapist from a young person's scorn but it holds back a young person's attempts to grow up and differentiate himself from his counsellor. So, like parents, counsellors have to allow this necessary process of disillusionment to happen in order for young people to grow up and rely on themselves rather than on other people. As I've said, self-disclosure ('Actually, this is what I'm really like...') can play an important part in this process.

But self-disclosure isn't appropriate with all young people: it depends on their readiness to start thinking about their counsellor as a real person. Telling a narcissistic baby about yourself would be pointless; a toddler might just about be able to start thinking about you as separate and individual. An older child might be slightly better able to do this, and a teenager better again. But there are some teenagers who are still effectively babies, and who, alone in a room with a counsellor, regress to a baby-state. I think that 15-year-old Flora was able to use my story. Had she been younger and still looking to me for simple reassurances, my story might well have been inappropriate. Had she been still absorbed in a narcissistic world and conversation of her own, she might have dismissed my story as entirely uninteresting, of no relevance to her. Most young people *are* interested in what their counsellor is 'really' like, however, and many will only be as real as their counsellor is real. The counsellor sets the tone. If the counsellor is evasive and aloof, stylized and strange, a young person will behave similarly.

Too much self-disclosure is potentially as unhelpful as no self-disclosure. Clarkson (1995) writes that, 'If all personal details are avoided in an embarrassed way, the client learns only to be careful of intimacy. If these are over-indulged in, the client can learn that he or she is less important than the psychotherapist…' (p.150). Self-disclosure is unhelpful if it overwhelms a young person's own material ('You think your life's hard? You should hear about *my* life!'). It's unhelpful if the young person is already progressing perfectly well without needing to know anything about the counsellor. It's unhelpful if, in some way, it deflects from the uniqueness of the young person's experience. It's unhelpful if the counsellor, feeling stuck, simply resorts to talking about himself rather than trying to work out what the young person really needs. And self-disclosure can sometimes be unhelpful when used to describe what's going on between the two people in the counselling room; when the counsellor describes what she's feeling towards the young person and what she imagines the young person is feeling towards her. For many young people, that's just *embarrassing* and exposing, however sincere or accurate it may be. A young person's readiness is all.

Callum bounces into my counselling room. 'Ha!' he gloats. 'I told you we'd win! Because we're the best! Because we're gonna win the league!'

I bow in mock surrender. 'I admit you played well, Callum. We didn't play that badly but you probably did deserve to win.'

'We definitely deserved to win!'

Six months ago, he'd have said, 'We definitely deserved to win because you're shit!', but we've made progress: Callum no longer feels the need to humiliate me on account of my football team's ineptitude; he no longer has to rub it in. Instead, he's able to enjoy his team's triumph at the weekend and my team's defeat without having to be personally antagonistic.

The fortunes of our football teams have allowed us to practise something important. When things have gone badly for my team, he's mocked me and I haven't retaliated. Instead, I've lamented my team's misfortune, smiled and borne the mockery. When his team has stumbled, I've teased him, but gently. He's learned to tolerate my teasing without feeling as if his life's at stake, as if he must fight back to maintain his dignity. Inevitably, these things resonate with Callum's life where, in the past, he's approached so many situations expecting to fight, expecting that people are out to get him. Because of the past, he has understandable reasons for approaching life in this way, but our conversations have allowed him to practise a gentler approach.

We both still refer to the other person's team as 'you'.

In counselling, every conversation needs to have some therapeutic purpose. I think that our conversations about football are entirely therapeutic. Sometimes they're a form of 'therapeutic foreplay' (Bramley 2014), a warm-up for more personal conversations; sometimes they're fun; sometimes they're playful; sometimes they're about what it's like to be fallible… Always they're part of the therapy. And if I hadn't told him which team I supported in the first place, none of this would have been possible.

17

Making Judgments

Laura looks worried, shuffling pages of case notes and telling me about a 15-year-old girl she's seeing. 'Obviously, I don't want to judge,' she says. 'She's determined to go back out with him, even though she knows perfectly well what he's like.'

I wonder what the future holds for the girl Laura's seeing, a girl going back out with a boy who, on several occasions, has hit her. I want to ask Laura what *she* thinks is behind the girl's seeming determination to stay with the boy, given the outrage at home when the girl finally admitted to her family that her bruises had, indeed, been inflicted by her boyfriend. I want to ask Laura what any of this might say about the girl's relationship with her father. Or with her mother as a role model. When she's with the boy, what's happens to the girl's anger? To her assertiveness?

'I'm really worried about what'll happen,' Laura says, agitated, 'but Becky has to make her own decisions. I know I can't say anything. It's not my place to judge.'

It's an interesting idea that a counsellor can ever be non-judgmental, that somehow Laura can be freed of moral perspective, of all personal points of view in order to sit with a young person like Becky and be 'non-judgmental'. Clearly, Laura thinks that it's not a good idea for Becky to go out with the boy again, but feels unable to say anything for fear of seeming 'judgmental'.

I ask, 'What would happen if you told Becky what you think?'

'I couldn't do that,' says Laura. 'It wouldn't be right to impose my views. That's not what I'm there for. Young people don't need other people judging them.'

'Don't they?' I say. 'I'm very judgmental!'

She looks disbelieving.

'I am! I can't help it. I hope that my judgments are tempered with compassion and understanding and often I keep them to myself. But they're always there!'

'Yes,' she says, 'but if you were me, you wouldn't be telling Becky what she should do with her life.'

'It would depend on what I thought she needed,' I say. 'I might well tell her what I thought if it was what she needed to know.'

Laura looks extremely doubtful. This isn't what she's been taught. I tell her that, in my experience, young people always want to be judged for doing good things, so whenever I think that they've done good things, I applaud them. Whenever they need the affirmation, I congratulate them on their successes, I admire their achievements, I delight in their happiness. I make no secret of my view because to greet all good things with po-faced neutrality would be weird.

All of which means that when young people have done bad, foolish or cruel things, I can't sit there and be po-faced either. Nor do young people want this. Often they're effectively saying, 'This thing happened… What d'you think?' They don't need a counsellor to reinforce their sense of personal badness, but often they need the containment of an adult saying that, yes, the behaviour was bad. We might then go on to think together about the anxieties provoking the behaviour in the first place, but together we'll acknowledge that it was, indeed, bad behaviour, however understandable the anxieties.

This matters because, in striving to be 'non-judgmental', there's a danger of counsellors ending up being bland, humourless and withholding: all the things young people don't need them to be. There's a danger of de-personalizing the relationship for fear of the counsellor's own personality or point of view obtruding. Laura insists that it's not her place to judge, and yet the reason counsellors go into rigorous therapy themselves is to understand where they end and other people begin, to take back their projections, if you like, seeing other people for who they are, rather than as narcissistic extensions of the counsellor. So professional counsellors ought to be able to judge what young people need at any particular moment without worrying about their own needs getting in the way.

Laura is scrupulous about not imposing her own views on young people and I respect this. She listens. She's kind. She wants to be helpful. She asks questions, trying to clarify what the young person is feeling. Eventually her session with the young person ends, but – I imagine – with the two most important questions still unanswered, questions the young person never actually asked but was wondering about throughout the session: unspoken, vital questions she hoped the counsellor would anticipate and find some way of answering: 'Am I mad? Am I bad?'

Containment doesn't just mean listening to everything. Sometimes containment (Bion 1963) means making sense of things and offering back an understanding, a story that makes sense, allowing the young person to leave the session knowing that 'I'm not actually mad. I may have made some mistakes and done some stupid things, but I'm not mad or bad. In fact, I make sense. At least to my counsellor!'

I share Lomas's (1994) view that 'the adoption of a moral stance cannot be avoided any more than the therapist can pretend to lack a body and have no emotions' (p.16), yet there's an assumption behind a lot of counselling practice that it's not appropriate for a counsellor to say what she thinks; that her job is, rather, to help young people arrive at their own understandings, which will develop organically; that the counsellor's job is to provide a supportive, non-judgmental context in which this will eventually occur. All of this is fine. The trouble is that most young people aren't going to stick around for long enough to get to it by themselves. They need their counsellor to be more proactive, more incisive. 'Am I mad? Am I bad? What d'you think?' If young people knew the answers, they wouldn't have bothered coming to counselling. For them, it might feel as if the world is spinning out of control, as if nothing ever stays the same except for an abiding sense that somehow they're getting it all wrong, that adults disapprove of them and that the future is horribly uncertain. So a young person like Becky decides to talk with a counsellor. She's never done this before. It's scary and, unsurprisingly, she finds herself worrying, 'Will my counsellor understand me? Will she disapprove of me? Will she make things clearer? Will she appreciate what my life's been like and what it feels like at the moment? Do I dare to tell her about the embarrassing things that have happened? About the times when I've messed up? About the foolish and unkind things I've done? I want my counsellor to like me and I want to know what she thinks, but at the same time I don't want her jumping in with lots of patronizing advice, making me feel stupid and childish.'

Counsellors are good at listening and they do plenty of that. They try to be impartial and let people arrive at their own evolving truths. But there are times when a young person needs to know what the counsellor actually thinks. Not just what the counsellor thinks the young person should do (most young people know perfectly well what to do, that's the easy bit) but what sense the counsellor makes of the young person's story. And, in particular, what answer the counsellor can give to those implicit questions, 'Am I mad? Am I bad?'

Laura's listening patiently to all this. 'So you're not saying that I should automatically tell Becky what I think. You're saying that it depends?'

'Exactly! Because there are moral judgments and clinical judgments,' I tell her. 'Your *moral* judgment might be that she shouldn't go back out with the boy again because she's putting herself in danger. Your *clinical* judgment might be that she needs you to keep quiet about that opinion. Or that she needs you to ask her about her father. Or about her mother. Or about something else… Your clinical judgment might be that she needs you to tell her your moral judgment, "I wouldn't go out with him, Becky, because it'll probably happen again!" Counsellors are always making clinical judgments about what to say, about how to say it and about when to say it; they're always judging when to give young people a steer and when to hold back… I think that you have to judge what Becky needs, Laura, and what your relationship with her can stand. How long have you been meeting with her?'

'Five months… Why?'

'Because that may be an important factor in what you decide to say. If this was the beginning of your relationship, you might well be judging that it's too early to say what you think, that Becky's still getting used to you, getting used to someone listening and being interested in her. But once she's begun to take that for granted, once she knows that you care and that you're not about to run off, she might be ready to cope with some feedback. It's like when a newborn baby suddenly needs its nappy changing, you accept that as you accept everything about the baby. You make no judgment…'

Laura looks alarmed.

'But if a toilet-trained child deliberately craps on your best sofa, you reprimand the child because the child knows better and has made a very bad decision! It wouldn't be fair to say nothing.'

'But I can't just say to Becky, '"Don't go out with him!"''

Laura's beginning to look fed up with her supervisor talking all the time, just as a young person would soon get fed up with a counsellor talking all the time. My guess is that, on the one hand, she wants me to be didactic so that she has a clear perspective, something to kick against, but on the other hand, she doesn't want to finish our supervision session with her confidence shredded, bullied by an opinionated supervisor and unable to think for herself.

I decide to risk one last bit of 'telling'. 'It's also a question of what exactly you say and how you say it, Laura. So instead of saying,

"Don't go out with him, Becky!", you might say something like, "I think you're in a really difficult position, Becky, and I can see why going back out with him would make sense because, like anyone, you don't want to lose a boy who *can* be really nice when he wants to be, even if he can also be a bastard. And like anyone in your position, Becky, you'll be worrying about what the future will be like without him. It's really hard to give up on people, even when we know that they might not right for us. Breaking up with someone is horrible, really horrible. The thought of never seeing them again, or of seeing them with someone else... And it's also horrible knowing that everyone's talking about it, as if they're the experts on your relationship. I think that, if and when you finish with him, Becky, it might well be the right thing to do, but it'll still be scary and upsetting. So I can see why you'd feel nervous about doing it..."'

Laura's laughing at me. 'You're so sly, putting it like that! You know perfectly well that Becky wouldn't be able to disagree if you said something like that to her!'

'She might well disagree,' I say, 'if I haven't understood her properly. And there'll be a lot to understand. Stuff about her life and about what this boy means to her. But that's all stuff you know, Laura. Stuff you can help her with. Really, you're offering her an *understanding* as much as a judgment because, as you know, no one changes their behaviour until their behaviour has been properly understood.'

'Oh God!' she says. 'I'd better write it all down and learn it off by heart before I say anything!'

I suggest that we practise right now in supervision. 'Imagine I'm Becky, and I'm saying to you, "Laura, please help me! I don't know what to do. Part of me wants to go out with him, despite what he's done. And I think I might love him. What d'you think I should do, Laura?"'

With no time to think, Laura's panicking.

'"Tell me what I should do, Laura! I really, *really* need your help! I need you to help me understand what's going on in my life! Help me! Tell me if I'm being stupid. What d'you think?"'

And because she's kind, because she cares and wants to help, Laura starts talking to Becky…

18

Playfulness

Josie sits down for an hour of supervision. I ask how things have been and immediately she starts telling me about a boy she's seeing. This would be fine – discussing him might well be a matter of urgency – except that she does this every time we meet: I ask her how things have been and, immediately, she starts telling me about a young person.

'We'll come to him in a minute, Josie. How have you been?'

She fends me off with a few banalities. 'Anyway, back to my boy,' she says as if she's having to teach me how to conduct proper supervision sessions.

She's studying for a counselling diploma, reading plenty of theory and sitting through lectures every week. At the same time, her life is changing with one child starting at university while another is in his last year at school. There's a lot going on in her life.

'Hang on, Josie,' I interrupt. 'We'll get on to talking about the boy, but your work with him will be partly informed by what you're reading and learning on the course, and by how you're feeling yourself at the moment… That's why I'm asking. I'm not asking to be nosy or to waste time!'

Josie does things by the book and the book presumably says that, in supervision, you discuss clients. She looks crestfallen now, as if she's made a mistake, displeasing her supervisor. 'What would you like to know?'

'Just how you are… How are things at home? How are things on the course? What are you reading? How are the kids? How are you feeling about life, the universe…?'

'Oh, I see,' she says. 'Fine, thank you. We had a lecture last week about ethics, which was really interesting. They gave us lots of case studies to think about…'

She looks at me as if to say, 'Will that do? Is that enough? Can we get back to discussing my clients now?'

Of course she's anxious and her greatest anxiety is to do a really good job on behalf of young people. But relentless intensity doesn't help those young people any more than relentless merriment. When Winnicott (1971) writes that 'psychotherapy has to do with two people playing together' (p.38), he doesn't mean people literally playing games together (although games sometimes have their place), but people being *playful* together: smiling, laughing, joking sometimes, sharing stories. His analogy is always with a mother and baby, with the mutuality of that relationship. We know from neuroscience (Gerhardt 2004) that if a mother's face is stricken and depressed, then her baby will absorb and, to some extent, become like that. Young people are likely to become a reflection of their counsellors, therefore. If the counsellor only ever responds to the client with a frown, then the client learns that his life is something to be frowned upon.

Young people typically come to counselling because something in their lives has got stuck: a relationship or a behaviour, a feeling or a thought, a part of themselves. They're hoping to become unstuck by talking with a counsellor who's consistent from session to session but who's also creative and spontaneous, a counsellor whose playfulness can free up the young person's stuckness.

Supervisors, in turn, are modelling for counsellors that same balance of consistency and playfulness. So, I wonder to myself, do I let Josie retreat back to her clients or do I push her to talk more about herself? Like anyone, she'll be defended for good reasons, and trying to strip away those defences will probably do more harm than good. She'll lose confidence if she thinks she's doing counselling the wrong way, but at the same time, she'll lose young people if she can't find a way to be a bit more playful. Somehow we need to practise that playfulness in supervision.

I decide to bide my time and let her tell me about the boy.

'He doesn't know what to do,' she says, 'because his mother's got MS and he thinks his father's having an affair with someone at work. Apparently his father says he's going off to meetings about work when really he's going to meet this woman, and Kian's found messages from the woman on his father's phone. So Kian doesn't know what to do because he doesn't want to upset his mother and doesn't want to make the situation any worse with his father.'

'He's stuck…'

'That's why he's come,' Josie says. 'He's not sleeping and can't concentrate on schoolwork because of worrying about everything at home.'

I ask her what Kian's like.

'He's a shy boy. Obviously, he loves his mother, but he's surprisingly loyal to his father.'

'And presumably furious with him?'

'He hasn't said that.'

'What's your guess, Josie?'

'Well, I suppose he could be angry inside,' she says, looking uncertain, 'but he's very shy so he doesn't really say too much about what he's feeling.'

'Have you asked him?'

'Not yet. I thought I'd wait and see what you thought.'

Counsellors can get just as stuck as young people, sometimes internalizing a young person's stuckness as if it were their own. It seems to me that Josie's boy is describing a particular stuckness: caught between loyalty to his mother and loyalty to his father; caught between whether to keep quiet or whether to shout and scream.

Alvarez (1992) describes a mother as a soothing but also 'enlivening' object: initiating play, arousing feelings, enjoying and delighting in her baby. My experience of Josie is that she gets stuck or *narrowed* in supervision: thinking about her clients' stories with great diligence and determination but without much joy, without much enlivenment. I imagine that, for Kian, counselling might feel like an equally joyless affair with nothing unusual ever happening and with his counsellor focused intently on trying to be a good counsellor, doing it by the book.

'It sounds important to find Kian's anger,' I say to her. 'We know that he can do loyalty and patience; we know that he's good at keeping quiet about things. It'll be important that he doesn't get stuck with those feelings, and that he doesn't get you feeling stuck as well, Josie. Remember that, apart from the situation at home, he's still a 13-year-old boy with all sorts of normal developmental things to negotiate, like sex and friends and enemies and separating from his parents and wondering about the point of anything. My guess is that he'll need you to be interested in the situation with his parents, but he'll also need you to be interested in his computer games or sports or pets or films or clothes or whatever else he likes... How much do you know about the rest of his life?'

'Not a lot,' she says defensively. 'He always wants to talk about his parents.'

'Well, ask him about the other things in his life as well. His parents are important – of course they are – but you have to be clear with him that he's much more than just a boy with difficult parents; he's interesting in all sorts of other ways as well...'

I can see her thinking to herself, 'Why? How's that supposed to help?'

'If we're only interested in their problems, young people are likely to identify themselves with their problems and not much else. "I'm the angry girl! I'm the violent boy! I'm the abused girl! I'm the dyslexic boy!" But if a counsellor starts noticing a wide range of interesting things about a young person, then he or she *becomes* a wide range of things and, in future, has more of a repertoire of possible responses when it comes to dealing with difficult situations.'

Josie says she agrees.

'That's why I often begin supervision by asking you how things have been in the last fortnight. Being a counsellor who listens attentively is only *part* of who you are, Josie. When you go into a room to work as a counsellor, *all* of you goes into the room. And all of you needs to be available to the young person in the room. Not just your attentiveness and empathy, but also your humour, your irreverence, your own adolescence, your silliness, your sadness…'

She looks abashed. 'Are you saying that I'm uptight?'

'I'm saying that, in striving to be a good counsellor, there's a danger of sticking rigidly to the official rules: starting and finishing on time, asking open questions, summarizing, getting people to talk about their feelings… All of them good things, but what young people want most of all…is you! They're not interested in theory or technique. They want a relationship that's personal. So I'm not saying that you're uptight but I *am* saying that some of the young people you're seeing might experience you as holding back a bit.'

She looks upset. 'How do you know I'm holding back? You're not there when I'm seeing people…'

She's right. I'm making an educated guess, based on the way she is in supervision. I say this to her.

'But for all you know, I might be very playful when I'm with young people!'

'Are you?'

She hesitates, thinking about this. 'Probably not enough.'

As counsellors become more confident, they become more playful, better able to hold in mind the therapeutic task while enjoying the company of a young person. And the therapeutic task will include enjoying the young person, being pleased to see him, liking him. Bramley (2014) describes the beginning of a counselling session as 'therapeutic foreplay'. 'Foreplay isn't only for, well, the fun of foreplay,' she writes. 'It has huge social and cultural relevance. Not only does its denouement ensure the species carries on – rape or intercourse without foreplay could achieve that. Successful foreplay leads to a deeper trustful bond such that – all other things being equal – the pair will remain together long enough to healthily rear, not just produce, the next generation. Foreplay is also about how to assist the partner to surrender control and control surrender (in other words be able to lose but find themselves again). We ought not to rape or seduce our clients or go straight into therapeutic intercourse without some foreplay, in other words adequate and sensitive acclimatization. If therapeutic foreplay isn't forthcoming, patients may well "freeze up" or just leave' (p.17).

I say all of this to Josie. 'So maybe what I'm suggesting is that you and I need to allow ourselves more time for supervisory foreplay!'

She looks horrified. Then laughs, 'You sound like a dirty old man!'

And somehow – between us – something shifts.

19

Sexuality in the Room

'It was the way he sat there and looked at me,' says Lucy, aghast. 'He was looking right at my legs and my chest. He didn't move at all, but I knew exactly what he was thinking!'

She's talking about 14-year-old Kieron who apparently sat opposite her in the counselling room and looked at her. Not in a hostile or intimidating way. But in *that* way.

'I didn't know what to do! I couldn't say 'Would you mind not looking at me like that, Kieron?' I couldn't think!'

I feel like saying to her, 'Get used to it, Lucy! If you're going to work with young people, they're going to bring sex into the counselling room whether you like it or not, and sometimes they'll fancy you. In fact, sometimes you'll fancy them!' But Lucy is new to this and shocked. I don't know whether the experience resonates with other experiences in her life. It'll almost certainly not have been covered on her training course… 'Eroticism in the Counselling Room: Discuss'. Counsellors sometimes talk about the eroticism of relationships with adult clients but it's much harder to talk about what goes on between a counsellor and a young person because all sorts of paedophilic anxieties arise (Luxmoore 2016): 'I'm much older than this young person. It's not right for me to have feelings about him or for him to have feelings about me. I shouldn't be feeling this way and I'm certainly not going to tell anyone about it!' But not acknowledging the sexuality implicit in *all* counselling relationships makes it more (rather than less) likely that something will go wrong and means that we block out a hugely important part of any young person's experience. If young people sense in their counsellor an anxiety about sexuality, they'll look elsewhere for those conversations and their experience of counselling will be diminished. So Lucy has a choice. She can shut down this part of her relationship with Kieron or find a way of living with it.

I ask, 'How surprising is it that a 14-year-old boy would look at a 30-something-year-old woman?'

'Very!' she says. 'Very surprising!'

'But Kieron probably goes home and masturbates, thinking about all sorts of people he's seen during the day. He probably watches lots of porn as well. Most boys are like that!'

Lucy looks as if she's swallowed a fly.

'They can't help it,' I go on. 'They wish they could, but they can't. It's biological. They've simply discovered this wonderful thing called "orgasm". And yet we so often shame them; we call boys "dirty" and "little"; we emasculate them. No sooner do they reach the milestone of puberty than we make it clear that we preferred them when they were children. We make it clear that we prefer girls with their neat handwriting, their ability to talk about their feelings and their interest in babies. The danger is that we fill boys with shame and with an anger that eventually explodes.'

Lucy looks crestfallen. 'You're making me feel sorry for him now!'

I say I'm glad. 'This is a boy, remember, with a violent father and a depressed mother. If ever he dares to assert himself at home, he gets threatened by his father and accused of making his mother's life a misery. So how's he supposed to learn to be appropriately sexual? To enjoy his sexuality? To be assertive without becoming a bully? To be passive without becoming a pushover?'

'You're *definitely* making me feel sorry for him now!'

'He might have fantasized about you, Lucy, but he didn't actually do or say anything wrong. He broke no boundaries. If he had, you'd have been absolutely right to tell him in no uncertain terms! Instead he looked, like a lot of men look. And it made you uncomfortable – fair enough – but if we now recoil in horror, we give Kieron the message that there's this horrible, bad, shameful part of him that no one wants to know about. Not even his counsellor. And sexual shame sometimes leads to sexual violence.'

I'm beginning to rant. Lucy says nothing.

'Imagine that you're Kieron, Lucy… You're alone in a counselling room with a woman who seems pleased to see you and who's clearly interested in what you have to say. She might be the only person in your life who takes an interest in you. You can't help noticing her body and imagining her with no clothes on. You've never had a girlfriend and you imagine what it would be like if she was your girlfriend, if you were having sex together. You remember some of the stuff you've seen on porn sites… You're Kieron, remember. You're 14 years old. In your heart, what are you hoping, Kieron?'

'That I can find a girlfriend?' says Lucy. 'Someone who'll love me? Who'll understand me?'

'And what are you afraid of?'

She frowns. 'That they'll find out about the stuff I do, like watching porn. And that I've never actually had a girlfriend, although I say I have. And that I've never had sex either. That secretly, I'm really nervous about all that stuff in case it turns out that I'm no good at it …'

'So, Kieron… You're seeing a counsellor called Lucy. I know you'd never say this in real life, but how do you need her to be with you, Kieron? Really?'

'I need her to keep things safe,' says Lucy, 'to stay in charge and tell me if I'm doing anything wrong. I need her to keep liking me and letting me talk about stuff. Especially about my mum and dad.'

'And if you ever wanted to talk with her about sex and things like that?'

'I'd need her to ask me. No way would I ever mention stuff like that!'

'And if she did ask you?'

'Then fine, I'll answer if I want. But I don't have to!'

Lucy's ability to become Kieron is impressive and reassuring: evidence of someone well able to empathize with what it's like to be a boy and to be 14. I ask what she's thinking.

'That it's pretty crap being a boy! And pretty lonely, really, keeping up a front all the time. Not letting anyone get close…'

'Which is why it's so good that he's daring to let you know stuff about him, and also why counsellors have to be so careful never to shame young people… Didn't you ever get a crush on any of your teachers at school?'

She laughs. 'One teacher! I remember we used to have competitions to see who could touch his jacket as he walked past during lessons!'

I tell her that I regularly compliment young people in counselling on how they look – new clothes, make-up, hairstyles – superficial things which say 'I've seen you and you look good' because I think the affirmation is important. Most young people are desperate for feedback as they nervously present themselves to the world. I've been shown clenched biceps by unconfident boys and have complimented the boys on how muscly they're becoming because it's as if they're always asking, 'Am I attractive? Do you think I'm attractive? Do you think there's any possibility that other people will think I'm attractive?' Developmentally, many young people get the initial affirmation they need from their parents. In Kieron's case, that sounds unlikely.

Lucy agrees. 'His dad tells him he's a little shit and his mum just ignores him.'

'So how can you indicate to him that you think he's an attractive person, without him getting the wrong idea?'

She makes a horrified face.

'You could be pleased to see him,' I suggest. 'You could enjoy his humour, be interested in his stories…'

'All of which I do already! He knows that.'

'You could think about sharing with him little snippets from your own life… A good film you watched, a mistake you made, a place you visited… You won't be turning him into a stalker but you'll be indicating that he's worth sharing these things with. Obviously, don't share with him anything you wouldn't want the whole world to know about, because Kieron won't keep your confidentiality! And be ruthless about starting and finishing on time so that he knows that the boundaries are still in place, that he may be special in his way but he's not becoming your special one.'

'What if he keeps staring at me?'

'Forgive him. Forgive him for being a boy. Forgive him for being sexual. Forgive him for getting it slightly wrong sometimes.'

'And what if he keeps on? What if he doesn't stop?'

'Then tell him very gently that it's not good to stare at people in case they get the wrong idea.'

Lucy looks a bit calmer. 'I'll do my best,' she says, 'but I'm not going to find this easy!'

20

The Durability Test

Fergus complains about a boy who comes to see him every week but blocks him at every turn. If Fergus asks Lennox how his week has been, Lennox says fine. If he asks how things are between Lennox and his parents, Lennox says okay. If Fergus presses, Lennox gets irritable, complaining that Fergus shouldn't be bothering to ask because everything's all right. If Fergus asks why Lennox is still coming to counselling, Lennox says he's coming because he's been told to come.

'But he doesn't *have* to come,' complains Fergus, evidently baffled. 'I've told him that it's not compulsory and he's certainly big enough and stroppy enough not to be doing something just because other people tell him to do it!'

I ask what Lennox is like.

'A bit intimidating, to be honest. Especially when he doesn't say anything. He stares at me sometimes like he really hates me, like he really doesn't want to be there. And yet he is!'

Fergus is well aware that young people are defended for good reasons and that counsellors must respect these defences while, at the same time, giving young people plenty of gentle opportunities to look at what their defences might be protecting. Understandably, some young people won't be able to make use of the opportunities – however gentle – because thinking about anything at the moment feels too difficult. 'People in pain cannot concentrate,' writes Josephine Klein (1995, p.99). And yet a few young people seem *willfully* defended, immutable, as if it's a matter of honour to keep counsellors and everyone else out.

'I don't know how much longer I can keep going,' says Fergus. 'It seems a bit pointless, me asking questions every week and him refusing to say anything about anything…'

Winnicott (1965) is right when he famously describes 'a child establishing a private self that is not communicating, and at the same time wanting to communicate and to be found. It is a sophisticated game of hide-and-seek in which it is a joy to be hidden but disaster not to be found' (p.186). Lennox might delight in his defences, in his ability to stay hidden, keeping Fergus out. Yet if Fergus were to give up on Lennox, abandoning the surly young man as a lost cause, Lennox would almost certainly be devastated, consigned to the very isolation he pretends to want.

Fergus has to persist. Young people are always ambivalent about being understood. In some ways it's what they long for: the relief of finally being understandable to another person, of being normal, not mad. 'Please understand me!' they seem to be screaming from the rooftops. And yet being understood brings losses as well as gains, because if other people understand, then they have some power; they've seen through to the vulnerability behind the defence. If other people understand, then it means that the young person is no longer so unique, so rare. Other people might now lose interest and forget about someone who's understandable. An understandable person might merge with all the other understandable people in the world: no longer extraordinary but ordinary like everyone else (Luxmoore 2011).

For many young people, therefore, being understood is both a threat and a relief. So how do counsellors work with young people who are very, very defended? Who come to counselling but come seemingly intent on resisting the counsellor's advances, however supportive those advances might be?

'You could offer him an understanding of what you think might be happening,' I say to Fergus.

'How do you mean?

'Well, without apportioning blame, you could describe the way you seem to be trying to help him and the way that Lennox, for his own good reasons no doubt, seems to be unable to use your help at the moment. You could say that you've noticed this happening and that you need his help in order to move things forward.'

'He'd say that there isn't a problem, that he's happy to keep coming because it keeps other people happy.'

'Which sounds like counselling might be his oblique way of punishing these other people. Who are they?'

Fergus sighs. 'His parents and social worker.'

'So maybe Lennox comes to counselling every week and says nothing as a way of taking revenge on them... He must be furious with them!'

Fergus agrees.

'What would happen if you suggested as much?'

'He'd deny it!'

'And then you'd be back to square one... What if you suggested that his behaviour makes complete sense, that we're always fighting back against people who try to control us?'

'He'd deny that he was fighting back against anyone!'

'And if you asked him to tell you more about his parents and social worker, about how he feels about them?'

'He'd just say that they're not important. That there's nothing to tell.'

I'm aware that Fergus and I are probably starting to re-enact what happens with Lennox: my every suggestion met with Fergus's defensive retort. I'm beginning to feel helpless and irritable in the same way, I'm sure, that Lennox manages to get Fergus to feel helpless and irritable: Lennox's feelings projected into Fergus.

'Maybe it would be good to try and empathize as accurately as possible with his situation?' I suggest. 'Not ask him questions inviting answers because we already know what the answers will be, but maybe just be thinking aloud, commenting on how annoying it is to be made to do things, how satisfying it feels to frustrate people, how scary it sometimes feels to be understood, how much safer it feels when no one understands…' I remind Fergus of Yalom's (1970) description of the 'Help-Rejecting Complainer', the person for whom any offer of help is always missing the point, any suggestion is always impossible, any strategy always doomed to fail. Yalom describes the frustration of working with the Help-Rejecting Complainer whose stuckness is as comfortable for the complainer as it's infuriating for everyone else. One strategy, Yalom suggests, is to change the rules of engagement. Instead of the therapist making endless suggestions only to be rebuffed, the therapist himself might take on the role of doom-merchant. 'You're right!' the therapist might say. 'Nothing will work for you. Your problems are far too difficult, far too complex. There really is no hope!' Hearing the therapist's apparent defeatism often provokes the complainer into switching roles. 'Oh well, I suppose there are *some* things I haven't tried,' she might say. 'There's probably *one* thing I could do…'

I suggest to Fergus that, if nothing changes, he might try this along the lines of… 'I think you're right, Lennox. There's probably nothing left for us to talk about. It sounds as if your life's going really well and you're living happily.'

This is sometimes called a paradoxical injunction. It's a high-risk strategy because a few young people might actually believe their counsellor's words and finish counselling immediately, but as a strategy, it often serves to jolt young people out of their stuckness.

'I'll see how the next session goes,' Fergus says, 'and I'll try that if nothing else is working.'

Two weeks later, we meet again and I'm keen to know how things have gone with Lennox. Did Fergus try the high-risk strategy?

'I didn't need to,' he says. 'It was weird because, almost from the moment he sat down, it was like there was something different. *He was different!* He actually started talking about stuff, like about how his parents embarrassed him in front of the social worker by going on about how he used to wet the bed when he was younger, and about how he thinks his mum might be having an affair. Real stuff! Oedipal stuff! Shame and sex! And I managed *not* to say that I thought he was behaving differently with me. We just talked…'

One of the perennial mysteries of counselling is the way in which things get talked about in supervision and then – for no obvious reason – something appears to shift in the counselling room. It's as if the supervisory conversation frees up something in the counsellor which is unconsciously communicated to the client, or which the client unconsciously tunes into. Either that, or counsellors get lucky sometimes! But it happens so often that it must be more than luck.

'Maybe Lennox was always testing you?' I suggest to Fergus. 'Maybe you had to pass the Durability Test?'

'Maybe,' he says. 'If so, it was a bloody hard test! I wouldn't recommend it to anyone!'

21

Self-Harming

'She used to do it a few years ago,' says Gail, 'and she's started again. Apparently various people have found out and told her that she should get counselling.'

For many young people – especially girls – the route to counselling is through self-harm. The adults in the young people's lives have noticed and are worried. The young people themselves are worried but need their counsellors to understand why self-harming makes sense, why it's hard to stop, and why stopping sometimes makes things worse (Spandler and Warner 2007). And, of course, there's always more to the story…

'She split up with her boyfriend a few months ago,' says Gail, 'and needless to say, he's been saying bad things about her. And her mum and dad's relationship isn't good. Her dad's been offered a new job which means moving, but her mum doesn't want to move. And Katarina *definitely* doesn't want to move! So things are pretty bad at home.'

In a few months' time, Gail tells me, Katarina will be 16 with exams beginning soon after her birthday. Her 13-year-old brother is autistic and her ten-year-old footballing brother is the apple of his father's eye. 'So, as you can see, she's got a lot on her plate. We've only had one session so far, and that was mainly me listening, trying to get the picture.'

I ask if Katarina said much about the self-harming.

'Not a lot. Only that she cuts sometimes and doesn't see why it's such a big deal.'

'What did you say?'

'Well, I agreed with her,' Gail says, looking at me warily. 'It sounds as if there are far more important things going on in her life.'

I share her view. It's easy to take self-harming at face value, as something bizarre and disturbing, rather than trying to understand it as symptomatic of something much more important, as the expression of strong feelings and as a way of coping that works, at least as far as the young person is concerned.

I ask Gail what she's left thinking about Katarina.

'I don't know,' she says. 'There's all this stuff going on in her life and maybe that's what we'll end up talking about... But I got this sense of her somehow being a bit distanced from it all, as if she was talking but observing herself all the time, not really *being* herself. Not really being *in* herself... Does that make sense?'

'As if she was going through the motions?'

'Definitely as if she was going through the motions,' says Gail, 'but as if her heart wasn't really in it...'

'Maybe that's the issue,' I suggest. 'Maybe her heart's not in it? Maybe her heart can't be in it for some reason? And maybe that's why she keeps herself distanced? Maybe cutting is as real as she gets?'

'Or maybe there's stuff that she's not telling me?' says Gail, thinking aloud. 'Maybe she's simply pissed off? If I was 16 with exams and a stupid ex-boyfriend and one autistic brother and another who was my dad's favourite and my parents were arguing all the time, I'd probably be so angry that I'd want to kill someone! So it might be a lot safer to detach myself from everything...' She pauses. 'I guess I'll have to wait and see. We've only had one session and I promised her that next time we'd talk more about the actual self-harming.'

'Because?'

'Because she said she wants to talk about it. She wants to stop but doesn't know how.'

I ask if Gail's seen the cuts. When young people say that they're cutting, some might be describing a few scratches on their forearms, while others are describing nasty gashes near their veins, gashes that require medical treatment. Unless the counsellor has seen the cuts, he or she can't begin to make a decision about whether the cuts require treatment and whether or not other people need to be informed. Because so many young people feel ashamed of what they've done, they're understandably reticent about showing their cuts. So sensitivity is all. But sometimes counsellors have to be pragmatists. Young people have to be kept safe, and there are times when other adults need to know what's happening. If a young person chooses not to show the cuts or if the cuts are on parts of the body that would be quite inappropriate for a counsellor to see, that's not necessarily a problem as long as they're shown to another responsible adult who can judge their severity.

I encourage Gail to inspect Katarina's cuts the next time they meet. 'Also, it makes it clear to her that you're not afraid of her cuts and of what they represent, that you're not afraid of her strongest feelings, however ugly or bloody they may be.'

'I know,' Gail says. 'I'm just never sure what to say when someone shows me what they've done. I never know how much attention to pay to the cuts themselves and how much to get back to the underlying issues. Katarina wants me to help her to stop cutting but she knows perfectly well that cutting isn't the real issue. The real issue is all the stuff that's happening in her life…'

The next time we meet for supervision, I ask how things have been going with Katarina.

'She says she hasn't cut recently,' says Gail. 'But after our last supervision I did have a look at the cuts and they weren't that bad – no fresh ones – so we decided not to tell anyone and agreed to see how things go.'

I tell her that she needs to keep looking. 'Just because a young person says that things are better now doesn't mean that they are.

Young people have to know whether you're still interested or just want an easy ride. Don't be fobbed off, Gail. Insist on seeing!'

'But that's treating her like a child,' says Gail, 'like I'm not trusting her to tell me the truth.'

She's right. But so am I. When it comes to potentially dangerous behaviour, counsellors can't mess about. A young person's safety might be at risk. So of course it's important to keep things in proportion; counsellors mustn't behave as if they're only interested in the symptoms, and they must be respectful of a young person's privacy.

'But there's a bottom line about safety,' I remind Gail. 'If a young person's going to be in danger, then to hell with privacy and confidentiality. You have to err on the side of safety, and if Katarina chooses to hate you for ever, then so be it!'

She looks irritated. This isn't what she wants to hear. 'So you're saying that I should look at the cuts, even if it messes up my relationship with Katarina?'

'Absolutely! But it almost certainly won't be as bad as that. Explain that you have a duty to keep checking because you care; that you know this is hard for her and that you respect her determination to deal with all the things that are happening in her life. Also, that you know cutting is only *one* of the ways in which she's dealing with these things at the moment. And that there's so much more about her life for you to understand…'

I ask if Gail herself has ever self-harmed.

'Never! I've never felt the need.'

'What, never? Never done anything risky? Never got drunk? Smoked? Never done anything you knew wasn't good for you? Never done things to yourself to spite other people?'

'When I was young,' she remembers, 'I did have a phase of pulling my hair out, after my youngest sister was born. But I stopped because my parents realized what I was doing and told me that they'd take away my dolls if I did it again!'

'So you stopped?'

She laughs. 'I didn't want to lose my dolls!'

I ask why she thinks she was pulling her hair out.

'I think it was because I was mad at my parents for having my sister. And at the time, there was this girl at school who was being horrible to me.'

'But you didn't tell your parents about any of that?'

'I couldn't!' she says. 'In our family you're expected to get on with life and not complain. You don't ask anyone for help!'

I point out that she's now become the person who helps other people.

'I know! I know! I've become the person I needed when I was young. Usual story! The person who helps girls when they're pulling their hair out…'

I'm unsure whether she's prepared to keep talking about this. 'So you stopped doing it because you didn't want to lose your dolls… What happened to your anger, Gail? What happened to all the stuff you were feeling inside?'

'I think I just became quite withdrawn for a while,' she says. 'Then things got better because we got this new teacher at school and the horrible girl started being nice to me. And at home… I don't know. I think I probably just got used to my sister being there.'

'But it's interesting that you became quite withdrawn. A bit like Katarina distancing herself from her life…'

Suddenly Gail sits upright. 'Cutting off from her life!' she blurts. 'Cutting off from her feelings. That's it!' She's looking pleased with herself. 'I think I've just made a connection… I've been worrying about whether I should be talking about the cuts or about all the other things that are happening in Katarina's life. But cutting might *be* her way of talking about her life!'

I'm trying to follow her train of thought and our time's already up.

She sees my bemusement. 'It's okay,' she says. 'I feel like I know what I'm doing now. Thank you! See you next time.'

She heads for the door and I still have no idea what she's thinking. Something about cutting being Katarina's way of talking about her life…

Two weeks later, we meet again. This time she's less excited but still pleased with herself.

'It was that metaphor about cutting,' she explains. 'Cutting off. Cutting through… I used it with Katarina and it seemed to make sense. We've really started talking about stuff. I did what you said and checked her arms and, fortunately, they were okay. And then I said something to her about cutting off from her feelings and that seemed to make sense to her. She says she cuts off from her anger and cuts off from her family. And about how cutting her arms makes her feel better… Everything was about cutting!'

I say I'm pleased that the work's going well.

'It is!' says Gail. 'Very well. Turns out that she's really, really upset about what happened with her boyfriend. That's the biggest deal. We're cutting the crap now!'

22

Making Sense of Fathers

'Bloody fathers!' says Janet. 'Every young person I'm seeing at the moment seems to have no father or an estranged father or a completely useless father!'

I share her exasperation. In counselling with young people, there's an endless supply of fathers who break promises, fathers who can't keep their trousers on, fathers who pretend to be the boss while behaving like the baby... Counsellors can develop very jaundiced views about fathers! And yet when young people *aren't* talking about their fathers, when they're talking about everyone else in the family and insisting that this person called 'father' is completely irrelevant, he invariably seems to be the missing link, the person who has to be accounted for somehow if sons and daughters are to develop a convincing sense of themselves because, like it or not, every young person knows that they partly owe their existence to this man. They have his DNA. He may have left home or may never have lived at home; he may have been a one-night stand or a sperm donor. Whatever the circumstances, the inescapable fact is that he exists and he's out there somewhere, walking around, thinking or not thinking about his child who's thinking or not thinking about him.

It's well documented that Freud, living in paternalistic times, makes the role of the father central to his theorizing, while Klein and Winnicott redress the balance, switching the therapeutic focus to the mother as the core of our unconscious experience. Against this theoretical background, mothers readily become the focus of so many conversations in counselling with young people, especially when there are no fathers living at home. It's easy to dismiss an absent or chaotic father as irrelevant compared with an ever-present mother.

Janet is understandably exasperated that 15-year-old Sonya won't let go of her relationship with her father. At every turn he disappoints, saying terrible things about Sonya, appearing only to be interested in himself and in his latest girlfriend. Yet still Sonya won't give up on him. Typically, she vows never to be hurt again and retreats for a few weeks. But then there's some communication between them and she's off again, agreeing to meet up with him despite everything that she knows.

'Why does she do it?' asks Janet. 'I mean, I know there's all that Oedipal stuff about fathers and maybe she's trying to claim him for herself. Maybe. But Sonya's not stupid. She knows what he's like! So why does she bother?'

It's a good question. Why *do* young people bother? After conception, what does a father contribute that a mother bringing up children on her own can't contribute? Does a second parent need to be a man? Shouldn't we be thinking instead of 'care-givers' whose gender doesn't matter? After all, if a young person is forever wrestling with love and hate, with good and bad, right and wrong, and if it suits that young person to split his parents into the one I love and the one I hate, the good one and the bad one, then a second parent on the receiving end of these projections doesn't need to be a man. A second parent just needs to be there and available as the object of a young person's idealizing and demonizing tendencies. Maybe Sonya can't give up on her father, maybe she can't consign him to outer darkness because she can't give up on the possibility that he might turn out – at least in part – to be good? So rather than simply split her parents into the good one and the bad one, maybe she's holding out for the possibility of her parents being a mixture of qualities about which she can feel appropriately mixed? And maybe that's a good thing? Maybe that's a mature thing?

'But it's also a self-destructive thing,' says Janet. 'Sonya's father causes her nothing but stress!'

I've sometimes wondered whether the point of fathers is their 'otherness' (Bollas 1989). If, developmentally, babies must move from a state of being physically and psychologically merged with their mothers to becoming separate from them, then I've wondered whether fathers provide the baby with an early and very obvious experience of otherness, of strangeness. 'There's this other person around and he's clearly not like my mother, so maybe in some ways I might not be like my mother?' Does a father's usefulness consist of the fact that – being male – he can represent otherness more obviously than another woman? And does this partly explain young people's enduring interest in their fathers as they grow up and try to define themselves in the world?

Janet's sceptical. 'We might well be curious about an alien species from the planet Man,' she laughs, 'but that doesn't mean that we'll necessarily have strong feelings about him. With Sonya, it's more than just curiosity. She's passionate about the idiot! She never stops talking about him and about their latest relationship disasters!'

I say that I've also wondered whether the point of fathers is that they provide us with models of separation. As children and later as young people, we watch our parents interact; we watch the way they come together and part, the way they can be fond of each other without having to be physically close the whole time. This is important information for sons and daughters grappling with their own experiences of merger and separation, of being alone in the world yet in relationship with other people. So with fathers who are leaving or who've left, I've wondered about the manner of their leaving and its effect on the young people observing. To what extent does a father's revelation that he's been having an affair and is leaving tonight serve as a template for young people? 'When the going gets tough or when you've made a mistake, just pack up your bags and run away!' To what extent do young people internalize the angry, violent, drunken separations that they witness? A father refusing to speak to a mother? Or a father begging to be allowed back? How much do these behaviours leave their mark on young people like Sonya and become the only ways they know of ending relationships, of separating from other people? After a father has left, how much do young people then start unconsciously re-enacting with a mother the manner of his leaving? Re-enacting the rows, the reconciliations, the threats and ultimatums? And if, for some reason, it's not possible to enact these things with a mother, how much do young people set about enacting equivalent scenarios with teachers, with the police or with other authority-figures in their lives, as if they're forever trying to make sense of an earlier experience, deciding how far to identify with a father's behaviour and how far to reject everything about him, doing everything differently?

'Some of that might be right,' says Janet, 'but you still wouldn't need the other person to be a man. And women have affairs as well. Women make mistakes. Women are sometimes the ones who leave...'

I ask what she knows about the way Sonya's parents separated.

'They split up when she was about nine because of her father's drinking and violence,' Janet says, 'and they've been fighting over money ever since. Sonya says it's got worse. Apparently in the beginning he used to come round for birthdays and things like that, but since he got his latest girlfriend it's been worse, and Sonya's mother won't have him anywhere near the house.'

I ask whether Sonya's behaviour towards her father might be some sort of re-enactment of the years since the split? Her attempt, perhaps, to maintain some sort of relationship with her father, the way her mother might once have attempted to maintain the relationship? Whether Sonya's behaviour represents her continuing attempt to see if the story might have a different ending or whether all relationships have to end acrimoniously?

'Maybe she just wants a father-figure in her life,' says Janet. 'Someone to stand up for her? Someone to protect her? Someone to play that role? It wouldn't have to be a man.'

In writing about fathers, Winnicott distinguishes between the 'co-nurturant' father who shares responsibility for love and affection, and the 'sire father' who takes on the role of physical protector, allowing the mother–baby relationship to develop under his watchful eye (Reeves 2013).

'Mind you,' Janet continues, 'you'd think that by now she'd have realized that she isn't going to get protectiveness from her father. Quite the opposite! But I suppose what we wish for and what we know from experience aren't necessarily the same thing. Sonya wouldn't be the first young person struggling to accept that a parent isn't ever going to change. Or maybe – if her life's chaotic, which it certainly is – there's a part of her hoping that he'll become some sort of disciplinary dad, reining her in? Maybe he's useful to her as someone to kick against if she can't kick against her mother?'

I agree with her. If parents take responsibility for rule-making, it frees young people to get on with their job of rule-*breaking*, of testing their strength, coming up against the frustrations of authority, of otherness traditionally characterized as paternal. 'He always says no! He won't let me do anything! He makes my life a misery!' If Sonya didn't have a father to kick against, she'd have to find one. A frustrating best friend, perhaps. Or a disappointing lover. Or some behaviour through which to explore her relationship with authority. She wouldn't necessarily need to replace her father with another man, but she'd need someone to hold the authoritarian role for her. Like a lot of lone parents, her mother could find herself playing both the 'nurturant' and the 'sire' roles, but it would be psychologically simpler for Sonya to have two separate people playing two separate roles.

I ask about Sonya's relationship with her father before the split.

'The usual thing,' Janet says, looking weary. 'When she was small, they were close. She was his princess … God, I hate that story!

It always ends badly. Girls always go from being Daddy's princess to Daddy's sworn enemy.'

She's right. So many girls tell that story about their fathers. 'Maybe she keeps meeting up with him as a way of trying to repair the damage?' I suggest. 'Maybe she's still grieving for the loss of that first relationship?'

'If that's right, then I suppose I have to let her grieve,' says Janet. 'But how can I help her do that without her always ending up getting hurt?'

'Perhaps it's a hurt she's familiar with?' I suggest. 'Perhaps it doesn't get any worse? Perhaps it's what she's always felt?'

Janet looks pained. 'Perhaps she's punishing herself for no longer being a princess?'

It's an interesting thought. How much are young people always doing that? Feeling that they've lost something that can never be recovered, feeling to blame for growing up? Freud (1923) might add something about fathers being associated with a 'death instinct', a censorious presence always threatening destruction, while mothers might be associated with a 'life instinct' giving birth to us. How much is Sonya therefore trying to appease a father whose disapproval, whose destructiveness she dreads as powerfully as she dreads dying? And as far as her counsellor Janet is concerned, what would therefore free Sonya from having to appease her father?

I remember a supervisee once observing that 'the impossible mother conceals the unavailable father'. It's an idea that fits so many situations; an idea that can be turned around ('the impossible father conceals the unavailable mother') and a reminder that perhaps mothers and fathers should never be thought of as separate entities. A father only exists because of a mother and vice versa.

'I wonder whether we're missing something,' I say. 'We're thinking about Sonya and her dreadful father, but perhaps we should be thinking more about the *triangle* of Sonya, her father and mother?

Perhaps Sonya's persistence with her father says something about her relationship with her mother?'

'Like what?'

'Like whether there's a part of her mother that's never quite given up on her father? Whether Sonya has unwittingly become the go-between, the expression of some unfinished emotional business between her parents? Or whether she persists with her father in order to punish her mother in some way? To show her mother how relationships *should* be done? Or to avoid being tied to her mother for the rest of her life?'

Lee (1997) suggests that children and young people whose parents have parted can find it harder to think in a joined-up, sequential, reflective way. Parents coming apart will feel like thoughts coming apart; the children of jumbled up parents will tend to think in a jumbled up way. By extension, a father physically and emotionally miles away might leave a daughter called Sonya feeling 'half-alive' (Seligman 1985), struggling to make sense of her life, to make connections, to hold her thoughts together.

'Perhaps Sonya holds on to her father because, unconsciously, she's trying to hold on to her capacity to think?' I suggest to Janet. 'There are so many young people in counselling whose parents have split up. Maybe they're all re-learning how to think in a coherent way?'

Janet looks unimpressed.

'Okay, but what if – at the very least – Sonya's persistence with her father was related to her mother?'

'As far as I know, her mother keeps out of it,' Janet explains. 'Apparently she says that if Sonya wants to have a relationship with her father, then that's up to her. Her mother won't let her father near the house but she never criticizes him or says what she really thinks.'

'Maybe that's the point,' I suggest. 'Maybe Sonya's only way of getting information about her father has been to keep meeting with him? If her mother was more forthcoming, it would allow Sonya to know where she stands, to make better sense of herself in relation to her parents. I think it would be worth pushing Sonya to try and find out more of her mother's side of the story in order to fill in the gaps. Then she might not need to invest so heavily in her father…'

Janet is an experienced counsellor, a good counsellor, noting down ideas as we talk. She knows that there's a lot more to say, that we're simply floating possibilities to hold in mind for the next time she sees Sonya, when they'll sit down together and, as ever, she'll ask Sonya how things have been.

23

Failure

Alice is a young person who's come to see me for counselling, saying that she's suffering from 'exam stress'. And so are her friends, she says. None of them are sleeping or eating properly. Some of them have even been to the doctor about it.

I feel sorry for her. She takes her life and her schoolwork seriously. She works hard. She tries her best. But with a few weeks to go before the dreaded exams, she's in a state: worrying all the time, sleeping badly, crying sometimes.

'I'm working in short bursts like they tell you to,' she says forlornly. 'And I'm trying to do nice things as well, like giving myself rewards. My mum and dad are really supportive. They're not pressurizing me at all. It's just me! I can't seem to stop worrying…'

I ask about the teachers at school.

'They're pretty stressed themselves,' she says. 'They're always going on about how we should relax, but you can see they're not relaxed! And then they do assemblies saying we should be doing at least four hours' work at night!'

Exam anxiety has existed for as long as there have been exams, as have all the other anxieties that occur whenever we want to do something well but are afraid of doing it badly. There's nothing new about this. We need a degree of anxiety to do our best; we need to be prepared, alert, ready. But what makes these experiences feel impossible and reduces perfectly competent people like Alice to tears is when no one helps us think about the possibility of failure.

In educational circles the f-word isn't mentioned. Alice will have sat through assemblies listening to famous people telling stories of wondrous success. Words like 'inspire' and 'inspirational' will have been used a lot. Sometimes Alice's own successes and those of her peers will have been applauded and rightly so. But, typically, her teachers will then have wrapped things up by saying to the assembled company something like, 'And so you see, anything is possible. There's nothing stopping you. You can achieve anything if you want it enough. Dreams can come true. It's only a matter of hard work and belief!'

No one will have put up their hand politely and asked in a tremulous voice, 'Sir, what if we work really hard and still don't get the grades?' No one will have dared to ask, 'Miss, how am I supposed to become the first female astronaut from this school when I'm really bad at maths and don't understand science?'

Hearing about other people's successes is all very well, but young people are more interested in hearing about other people's failures. They want to know about all the things that went wrong, the mistakes, the stupidities, the misunderstandings, the personal limitations. They have strong feelings about people with disabilities, for example, because the notion of disability feels so personal: 'What about all the things *I* can't do? All the things *I'm* no good at? The things I'll *never* be any good at?'

The rhetoric of Success! Success! Success! has invaded schools as it's invaded other areas of life, encouraged by 'inspirational' business leaders, 'aspirational' politicians and 'positive' psychologists. Alice and her stressed-out friends are implicitly asking important questions of the people around them: 'What if we fail? What will we be worth then? How will we understand ourselves?'

Schools have bought into the rhetoric that everything is possible because no one dares to tell young people the truth: that everything *isn't* possible. 'Failing' schools allegedly fail to inspire young people and no one wants to be associated with a 'failing' school. So the language of 'inspiration' ('Success! Success! Success! You can do anything!') has become obligatory. The possibility of failing has become unmentionable, unthinkable. Tucker (2015) argues that society's anxieties are projected onto schools that are then punished for failing to make those anxieties disappear. He describes research into schools where 'The fear of failure appeared to drive individuals to greater and greater efforts, even when these appeared unrealistic or damaging to the self' (p.258).

I once worked in a school where our exam results improved, year after year. I was as pleased as anyone but couldn't help noticing that, year after year, we seemed to become more and more anxious. It was as if we'd all bought into the myth of relentless improvement, the belief that as long as we continued to try our very best, our results would continue to improve and we'd get our just desserts. Yet the increasing levels of anxiety in the school hinted at what we knew only too well: that continued success wasn't going to be possible. There would come a time…

When the time did come, as it was bound to do, the school actually avoided publishing its results, claiming that there was so much exam board re-marking going on that it would be misleading to publish any results in the near future. Clearly, the shame of our apparent 'failure' was too much.

I think that the anxiety or 'stress' described by so many young people like Alice is born of the realization that the institutional rhetoric about success is no longer to be trusted and that another outcome is equally possible, an outcome apparently so dreadful that no one will even talk about it.

I ask her what it would be like to fail her exams.

'Awful,' she says. 'I don't know what I'd do. I suppose I'd get over it eventually but it wouldn't be nice.'

'It certainly wouldn't be nice,' I agree with her. 'And you're right. You would get over it, Alice. You'd survive.'

'Yes,' she says, thinking, 'but…'

'But?'

'I don't know. It just wouldn't feel right. I'd feel like I'd let everyone down. Or like I wasn't being myself any more. I know that might sound a bit weird but I don't know how else to say it.'

Alice's sense of herself may have become founded on the idea of being Successful Alice but failure and disappointment are with us from the moment we're born. Our relationship with a mother never lives up to the blissful union that we half-remember from before birth. She turns out to be imperfect. A father's attention becomes erratic once the novelty of a new baby has worn off. And siblings are always a mixed blessing. From birth, we start the lifelong, developmental process of bearing disappointment and bearing the frustration of things never being as good as they could be (Phillips 2012). In a sense, we spend our lives wrestling constantly with our potential to fail, with our essential ordinariness (Luxmoore 2011).

So when someone comes along with a promise of certain success, we grab at it, keen to believe that our experiences of disappointment and failure might have been temporary all along and might now be banished for ever. Perhaps we've just been unlucky! Perhaps, in the new future, we'll all be successful, no longer tarnished by failure! Like some of their parents and teachers, Alice and her friends have developed 'false selves' (Winnicott 1965), defending them against the hurts of failure. I don't blame them. It's hard for parents who love their children to admit to being less than perfect. It's hard for teachers who care about their students to admit that they can't do it for all of the people all of the time. 'At an unconscious level,' writes Obholzer (1994), 'what is hoped for from the education system is unreality: that all our children will be well-equipped – ideally, equally equipped – to meet all of life's challenges' (p.172).

There's a sense in which young people always come to counselling to find out whether success really will be possible or whether failure and compromise are inevitable: 'Why did my boyfriend break up with me? Why are my friends so difficult? Why can't I get a part-time job? Why do I have to look like this? Why did bad things happen in the past? Why can't there be happy endings?' Young people come to counselling to learn about failure because, whereas absolute triumph might be possible in a race or in a computer game, relationships will always be a mixture of triumph and disaster. In that sense, relationships will always be about failure, at least in part. And counselling relationships will be no different. Counselling doesn't make the pain go away. Counselling doesn't mend broken hearts or bring people back from the dead.

Alice asks if I know any good tips for passing exams.

'Nothing you won't have thought of already,' I tell her, 'because exams are always difficult. We do our best and sometimes we fail. And the exams don't stop once we leave school or university. We carry on facing difficult challenges throughout our lives, and we carry on worrying that we'll fail.'

'Thanks!' she says, joking. 'You're really cheering me up!'

Because schools defend against the very thought of failure, young people are left to make sense of the experience for themselves, often without support. For those unused to failure of any sort, the experience can be crushing, as if everything has suddenly fallen apart, as if nothing will ever be the same. Conversations about failure are therefore central to the task of counselling: conversations acknowledging not just the possibility but the *inevitability* of failure, conversations detoxifying failure, taking away the shame of failure, making failure normal.

Alice and I will go on to talk about the dreams that her parents might once have had, and about the ways they might have learned to live with life as it is, rather than as they might have liked it to be. We'll talk about life always being a mixture of the good and the bad, the successful and the unsuccessful.

Encouraging young people to think only of success encourages them to split off the possibility of failure in the way that a baby or child might learn to split the bad from the good, the hateful from the loveable. Like all defensive splitting, it serves a purpose but is ultimately unsustainable once a child becomes a young person and senses that the world is no longer so simple. I think that Alice and her friends are sensing this, however much their teachers might still be pretending otherwise. Their suspicions leave them feeling very anxious.

'You're right about me not cheering you up,' I say to her. 'In fact, it's worse than that! I'm the bearer of even more bad news! Sometimes life sucks. Sometimes we don't get what we deserve. Sometimes bad things happen to good people...'

'I know,' she says. 'I do know that! It's just that...'

'That it's not fair?'

'Yeah!'

On the wall of my counselling room I have this quotation from the playwright Samuel Beckett: 'Ever tried. Ever failed. No matter. Try again. Fail again. Fail better', and in my diary, I keep this quotation from the autobiography of Richard Holloway (2013), an Anglican priest who lost his faith. 'This is grace,' he writes. 'Unearned undeserved unconditional acceptance of unchanging failure, including biological failure, our last failure, our dying' (p.253).

The acceptance Holloway describes has nothing to do with lazy under-achievement or with not caring. And Beckett isn't suggesting that success will be just around the corner. They're both describing a much more personal experience of our limitations. We try our best. We do. And we fail all the time because we're people. For young people, this is liberating rather than demoralizing.

24

Existential Answers

It's what so many young people say in response to accidents, deaths and other misfortunes. I ask what sense they make of whatever it is that's happened. What was the purpose? What was the point?

'I don't know,' says the young person, 'but I think that everything happens for a reason.'

We pick away at this, wondering whether natural disasters and human cruelties happen for a reason, whether a relative's cancer happened for a reason. And if there was a reason, what was it? Who decided on the reason?

'Everything happens for a reason' describes an illusion of intentionality, a world organized and joined up, a world that makes sense because someone somewhere is arranging things, making sure that it makes sense. It's an illusion that needs to be challenged because – unchallenged – the consequences for young people can be dire.

Young people are forever wrestling with a sense of agency, with what they can and can't control in the world, with whether accidents are ever really accidents. They're wrestling with predestination, free will, fate, freedom and the nature of personal responsibility. Sometimes they believe that they can control everything and, at other times, that they can control nothing. It's hard for them to accept that they might be able to control some things and not others when Education is offering a different possibility: 'Work hard! Work harder! Work even harder,' says Education, 'and you'll get to control everything in your life!' The implication is that life can be controlled through education, through religion, money, technology and a thousand consumer products. 'Everything happens for a reason' in a well-organized, fair, predictable world. The mantra denies that some things might happen for no reason, that they might be 'random' (a word young people are fond of using). So when the really big things happen – disasters, genocides – it's comforting to believe that there's a purpose behind everything, that it's possible to make meaning out of apparent meaninglessness and futility. But when the smaller, everyday things go wrong – when there are no jobs to be had, when lovers break up, when families fight – it's much harder to believe the mantra because these are the things over which young people expect to have control. They've worked hard in school and still there's no job; they've tried their best and still their lover leaves them; they've helped out at home and still their parents are quarrelling.

When young people expect to have control and find that they have none, 'everything happens for a reason' becomes unsustainable, and that's when young people become dangerous, likely to take revenge on themselves, on other people or on a world for seemingly breaking a promise. When they say that everything happens for a reason, they need to be challenged gently and sympathetically. It doesn't matter if counsellors don't have the answers, but it does matter that they keep asking the questions because sometimes the alternative for young people, clinging to the illusion of control, is a catastrophic disillusionment (Luxmoore 2012).

Officially, Gillian comes to see me for supervision, to talk enthusiastically about the young people she's working with in counselling, but she also wants to talk about her mother who's dying: about the sadness of it all, about feeling guilty for resenting her mother, about what life will be like after her mother's death, about the sheer inconvenience of everything happening right now, just as she's busy with work and with her own children.

'Mum hasn't had a good week,' she says. 'The staff at the home are very good but you can see them thinking that there's not long to go.'

I say that I'm sorry to hear this.

'It's okay,' she says. 'It's just one of those things. Sod's law. Nothing anybody can do. We all have to get on and get through, and fortunately, my sister's coming back from America, so she's going to be around to help if I'm caught up with work.'

I ask how work has been.

'Annoying! I've found myself feeling really irritated with everyone. With people in the office, with the other counsellors. And irritated with most of the young people I'm seeing who don't seem to be making any progress at the moment. Who don't seem to *want* to be making any progress!'

I ask her to say more.

'They just seem to think that counselling is this nice conversation they can have once a week where they don't have to do any real thinking. They can just keep me happy with an update on whatever's been happening and that's it. Job done! See you in a week's time!'

I say that they sound like staff in a care home.

She thinks about this. 'They do! That's exactly what the staff in my mother's nursing home are like. But they're doing their jobs, whereas the young people I'm seeing are avoiding doing theirs!'

We both smile.

'Maybe the young people are picking up something about you at the moment, Gillian, and trying to be nice to you, trying to protect you?'

'From what?'

'I don't know… From thinking about the future? From thinking about death?'

'But they don't know anything about my mother,' she says. 'I deliberately haven't told anyone except the manager of the counselling service and you.'

'That might not stop them knowing unconsciously,' I say. 'They might sense something and be only too happy to avoid all that existential anxiety. Unconsciously it might suit them.

Remember, when conversations go flat and nothing much seems to be happening, it's always worth wondering whether something's being avoided.'

'I know that,' she says, thinking about this. 'Oh shit! So you think it's me who's the problem?'

'Not the problem,' I assure her, 'but as you know, lots of adults assume that young people don't want to talk about these things – about death, about the meaning of life – so it easily becomes a blind spot. I'm sure that all the young people you're seeing will have their existential anxieties, their existential questions. They'll all need to talk about these things at some point... Why was I born? What's the point of living if we're all going to die? What's the point of relationships? Why should I bother?'

'Hmm,' Gillian muses, 'that's exactly what one of my girls – Kara – says. "Why should I bother? Why should I care?" She says it about school, about her exams, about having to do things at home...'

'And what do you say?'

'I suppose I ask her about relationships at school and at home. I don't ask her about the meaning of life.'

'Well, ask!' I say. 'Ask all of them about the meaning of life! Especially the ones who are irritating you. "Why should I bother?" is a really good question for a young person to be asking. "Why should I bother with my exams if I'm only going to get average grades? Why should I bother with my mother if she's going to die?" You don't have to have answers, Gillian. You just have to acknowledge that these are really good questions and that it's really hard for any of us to work out the answers.'

'I think that's the trouble,' she says. 'I don't have the answers. And I agree with them about the unimportance of exams!'

'So why are you bothering with your dying mother?'

'Because I love my mother,' she replies, mildly indignant, 'and because she'd have done exactly the same for me if I'd been ill or dying. Because it's what we do as people. We look after each other. It's why we're counsellors, after all!'

I agree with her. 'And if you said all of that to a young person and *still* he or she continued to ask why, "*Why* do we bother to look after each other in the first place?", what would you say? In counselling, young people are always asking us, in effect, "Why was I born? I didn't ask to be born! Why should I take responsibility for my life?"'

Gillian looks worried.

'You really don't have to have the answer. You can say that you don't know…or that you're still trying to work it out. Which is usually reassuring for young people who are also trying to work it out and who need to know that *not* having worked it out is okay. If they think they're supposed to have the answers by now, that's when they come up with stuff like "Everything happens for a reason" which often just closes down the conversation. Counsellors are allowed to be philosophical, Gillian. And young people are *very* philosophical! Coming to counselling might be a roundabout way of getting to have a philosophical conversation with an adult who takes the young person's questioning seriously.'

'Okay,' she says. 'Next week, I promise, I'll bring it into *all* my conversations.' She pauses. 'I don't suppose you've got any answers, have you?' She sits back and smiles to herself. 'No, I didn't think so!'

25

Endings

It's our penultimate supervision meeting. By the time we meet again, Tanya will have finished with half the young people she's currently seeing because, having done their exams, they'll be leaving school.

I ask how she's feeling about saying goodbye to them and about how the endings have been going.

'Bit of a mixture,' she says. 'Rowan said he didn't need to come any more and I've had a couple of other people who haven't turned up. But the rest are muddling through. It's been difficult for them with their exams and never knowing when they're going to be around. I guess they've all got a lot on their minds...'

A few months ago, I suggested to her that, because of the practical messiness of the exam season, it might be a good idea to finish with people sooner rather than later; that once the exams had started, it would be difficult for the young people seeing Tanya to attend their counselling appointments.

'But they're all panicking about the exams!' she replied at the time, perturbed. 'My sense is that they're going to need the counselling space even *more* during the exams in order to get through. Especially the most vulnerable ones.'

'They'll need it if you offer it,' I remember saying. 'If you don't offer it, if you assure them that they'll be fine during the exams, then they probably *will* be fine. And besides, they've got plenty of other members of staff in school to support them.'

But Tanya wasn't convinced.

I've written about the importance of endings that allow young people to go off and re-attach elsewhere without clinging to the hope that their old relationships will somehow be restored to them (Luxmoore 2000). But I've also written about the inevitable messiness of endings with young people where so many practicalities and mixed feelings interfere with a counsellor's careful planning (Luxmoore 2008). As Murdin (2000) points out, feelings about an ending are more easily avoided if the people involved have somewhere to go next and, for most young people, there's usually somewhere to go next.

Tanya has chosen to hold on to her clients during their exams in the belief that they'll 'need the counselling space even more'. I wonder to myself how much she might be needing to hold on to them as much as they need to hold on to her. Again, I ask how she's feeling about the prospect of saying goodbye to the young people she's been supporting for months and, in some cases, years; young people about whom she cares.

'You mean, how am *I* feeling?'

'Yes, how are *you* feeling?'

She doesn't know, she says, which sounds honest. This is the first time Tanya's had to say goodbye to so many young people all at once. It's a new experience. She'll probably never see any of them again and must somehow face this reality without becoming either coldly mechanical ('They're just another bunch of young people!') or hopelessly bereft ('I can't bear the thought of never seeing them again!').

It's a reality that the young people themselves are facing: 'Should I cut myself off from school and all that it represents, telling myself that I don't care? Or should I cling to school for all I'm worth and pretend that I'm not really leaving?' As they come towards the end of a counselling relationship, especially when the counselling relationship matters and especially when it coincides with the end of their relationship with school, young people are faced with a whole set of existential questions... 'What's the point of having relationships if they always end? Will anyone remember me? Am I worth anything? Does love really exist or are we just a selfish species intent on survival? What's the point of doing anything in life if we're all going to die?' These are really good questions which preoccupy young people far more than is popularly supposed (Luxmoore 2012). They're questions that need to be addressed in counselling, particularly when the end of a counselling relationship is in sight. They're not 'morbid' questions but vital questions that young people *should* be asking and that counsellors *should* be addressing without feeling that they need to supply answers.

However, some counsellors are understandably reluctant to engage with these questions because of their own existential anxieties. 'I've cared about all these young people... Why? To what end? What was the point when I'm never going to see them again and when some of them will go on to experience unhappiness in their lives despite all my efforts? Will I have made any difference? Does my work matter? Do I matter?'

In the film *Goodbye, Mr. Chips*, originally made in 1939 but since remade several times (always a sign that it taps into something important), the eponymously benevolent teacher gets older but his pupils never seem to age ('I taught your grandfather!'). His pupils and their children are always returning to say thank you to their old teacher and to the school that's become a god-like container in the background of their lives, keeping them safe. Even when various alumni are killed in the First World War, despair is never countenanced by Mr. Chips. Life goes on and life is fundamentally kind.

However, the novella on which the film is based (Hilton 1934) tells a less rosy story. In the novella, Mr. Chips is thinking about his many ex-pupils and wondering what's become of them, scattered now around the world, some of them probably happy, some of them probably not. He notes the 'strange randomness' whereby nothing can ever be the same again. His relationships with the pupils can never be revived. They are lost to him, the meaning of their lives and the meaning of his part in their lives unclear. This, I would suggest, is closer to most counsellors' experience: a cumulative sense of loss as, year after year, they say goodbye to so many young people. Like teachers, counsellors say goodbye never knowing how the story will end. Some young people will go on to wonderful things, but others won't. Despite the counsellor's best love and best efforts, day after day after day, he or she knows that some young people will still have unhappy lives. Counselling may have protected some young people from the vicissitudes of life but that protection has now ended. They're on their own.

Without making attachments, nothing very worthwhile is ever achieved by counsellors. But attachment is also the mechanism that leaves counsellors vulnerable. Some protect themselves with jokes and cynicism; some insist on simple behavioural solutions to human problems in the hope that this will keep them untouched and unhurt by relationships. But for conscientious counsellors, emotional withdrawal isn't an option. 'Epistemic trust' (Fonagy and Allison 2014) describes the way in which a young person's ability to learn depends on his or her ability to attach to (and therefore trust) the person teaching. For counsellors and for young people, it has to be personal as well as professional, therefore. And yet, year after year, counsellors like Tanya must say goodbye, knowing that they haven't been able to do it for all of the young people all of the time, that they've been necessarily imperfect. Year after year, it's hard to bear this. It's tempting to retreat into bureaucracy and protocols. It's tempting to retaliate ('You're abandoning me, so I'll abandon you!'). It's tempting to give up.

'You'll probably never see them again,' I say to Tanya. 'You'll never know how the story ends…'

She nods slowly, thinking about this.

'They'll always talk about keeping in touch; they'll say things like "See you around, Tanya!" So maybe it would be good to get them thinking about the fact that, realistically, they *won't* see you around.

It might be very important for them to confront the fact that an ending is an ending is an ending…'

We pause.

'It'll certainly be sad,' she says. 'I'll miss them.'

'And by all means say that to them, Tanya. But don't fudge the ending. Get them asking those big existential questions! Help them bear the anxiety of not having answers… What's the point of relationships? Why does everything have to end? Why don't we just give up?'

She smiles at me. 'You're in a cheerful mood!'

We both laugh. I remind her that this is also our penultimate supervision meeting because, as she's known for a long time, I'm leaving my job. In a fortnight, we'll be meeting for the last time.

'Another ending!' she says.

There's silence between us.

I ask what she's thinking.

'I'm thinking back to when we started and when I was new here and still learning everything… It seems a long time ago. A lot's changed.'

I say that she's a confident, skilled counsellor now.

'It doesn't always feel like that,' she says hurriedly. 'But it'll be strange not meeting for supervision any longer.'

'It will be strange,' I agree with her. 'I'll miss seeing you. I'll miss hearing about your clients and about how you're getting on.'

'But we'll still see each other at conferences and things,' she says.

'We will, but it'll be different,' I say. 'I'll no longer be your supervisor and you'll no longer be my supervisee. If and when we meet, I won't ask you about your clients and won't expect you to tell me about them.'

'Hell!' she jokes. 'What'll we talk about?'

We look at each other, neither of us entirely sure.

References

Alexander, L. (2012) 'The Adolescent, the Therapist and the School Environment.' In A. Horne and M. Lanyado (eds) *Winnicott's Children*. Hove: Routledge.

Alvarez, A. (1992) *Live Company: Psychoanalytic Psychotherapy with Autistic, Borderline, Deprived and Abused Children*. London and New York, NY: Tavistock/Routledge.

Association for Young People's Health (2015) *Key Data on Adolescence*. London: Association for Young People's Health.

Bion, W.R. (1961) *Experiences in Groups*. London: Tavistock Publications.

Bion, W.R. (1963) *Elements of Psycho-analysis*. London: Heinemann.

Bollas, C. (1989) *Forces of Destiny: Psychoanalysis and Human Idiom*. London: Free Association Books.

Bond, M. and Holland, S. (1998) *Skills of Clinical Supervision for Nurses*. Buckingham: Open University Press.

Bramley, W. (1996) *The Supervisory Couple in Broad-Spectrum Psychotherapy*. London: Free Association Books.

Bramley, W. (2014, December) 'Serious play and playful seriousness: Implications for psychotherapy.' *Bulletin 60. The Oxford Psychotherapy Society*.

Casement, P. (1985) *On Learning from the Patient*. London: Tavistock Publications.

Clarkson, P. (1995) *The Therapeutic Relationship*. London: Whurr Publishers.

Davies, J. (2013) *Cracked: Why Psychiatry Is Doing More Harm Than Good*. London: Icon Books.

Fonagy, P. and Allison, E. (2014) 'The role of mentalising and epistemic trust in the therapeutic relationship.' *Psychotherapy 51*, 3, 372–380.

Fonagy, P., Gergely, G., Jurist, E.J. and Target, M. (2004) *Affect Regulation, Mentalisation, and the Development of the Self*. London: Karnac Books.

Freud, S. (1923) 'The Ego and the Id.' In *The Standard Edition of the Complete Psychological Works of Sigmund Freud (Vol 19)*. London: Hogarth Press.

Gerhardt, S. (2004) *Why Love Matters: How Affection Shapes a Baby's Brain*. Hove: Brunner-Routledge.

Glasser, M. (1979) 'Some Aspects of the Role of Aggression in the Perversions.' In L. Rosen (ed.) *Sexual Deviation*. Oxford, New York, NY, and Toronto: Oxford University Press.

Grinberg, L. (1997) 'On Transference and Countertransference and the Technique of Supervision.' In B. Martindale, M. Morner, M.E.C. Rodriguez and J-P. Vidit (eds) *Supervision and Its Vicissitudes*. London: Karnac Books.

Hawkins, P. and Shohet, R. (1989) *Supervision in the Helping Professions*. Buckingham: Open University Press.

Hilton, J. (1934) *Goodbye Mr. Chips*. London: Hodder Paperbacks.

Holloway, R. (2013) *Leaving Alexandria*. Edinburgh: Canongate Books.

Hurry, A. (1998) 'Psychoanalysis and Developmental Theory.' In A. Hurry (ed.) *Psychoanalysis and Developmental Theory*. London: Karnac Books.

Kernberg, O.F. (2012) *The Inseparable Nature of Love and Aggression*. Washington, DC, and London: American Psychiatric Publishing.

Klein, J. (1995) *Doubts and Certainties in the Practice of Psychotherapy*. London: Karnac Books.

Klein, M. (1957) *Envy and Gratitude: A Study in Unconscious Sources*. London: Tavistock Publications.

Kohut, H. (1971) *The Analysis of the Self*. New York: International Universities Press.

Lee, G. (1997) 'Alone Among Three: The Father and the Oedipus Complex.' In V. Richards and G. Wilce (eds) *Fathers, Families and the Outside World*. London: Karnac Books.

Lomas, P. (1987) *The Limits of Interpretation*. London: Constable.

Lomas, P. (1994) *Cultivating Intuition*. London: Penguin Books.

Luxmoore, N. (2000) *Listening to Young People in School, Youth Work and Counselling*. London: Jessica Kingsley Publishers.

Luxmoore, N. (2006) *Working with Anger and Young People*. London: Jessica Kingsley Publishers.

Luxmoore, N. (2008) *Young People in Love and in Hate*. London: Jessica Kingsley Publishers.

Luxmoore, N. (2011) *Young People and the Curse of Ordinariness*. London: Jessica Kingsley Publishers.

Luxmoore, N. (2012) *Young People, Death and the Unfairness of Everything*. London: Jessica Kingsley Publishers.

Luxmoore, N. (2014) *School Counsellors Working with Young People and Staff: A Whole-School Approach*. London: Jessica Kingsley Publishers.

Luxmoore, N. (2016) *Horny and Hormonal: Young People, Sex and the Anxieties of Sexuality*. London: Jessica Kingsley Publishers.

Murdin, L. (2000) *How Much is Enough? Endings in Psychotherapy and Counselling*. London: Routledge.

Obholzer, A. (1994) 'Managing Social Anxieties in Public Sector Organisations.' In A. Obholzer and V. Zagier Roberts (eds) *Individual and Organisational Stress in the Human Services*. London: Routledge.

Obholzer, A. and Zagier Roberts, V. (eds) (1994) *Individual and Organisational Stress in the Human Services*. London: Routledge.

Phillips, A. (1994) *On Flirtation*. London: Faber.

Phillips, A. (2012) *Missing Out: In Praise of the Unlived Life*. London: Hamish Hamilton.

Reeves, C. (2013) 'On the Margins: The Role of the Father in Winnicott's Writings.' In J. Abram (ed.) *Donald Winnicott Today*. Hove: Routledge.

Szecsody, I. (1997) 'Is Learning Possible?' In B. Martindale, M. Morner, M.E.C. Rodriguez and J-P. Vidit (eds) *Supervision and Its Vicissitudes*. London: Karnac Books.

Seligman, E. (1985) 'The Half-Alive Ones.' In A. Samuels (ed.) *The Father: Contemporary Jungian Perspectives*. New York, NY: New York University Press.

Spandler, H. and Warner, S. (eds) (2007) *Beyond Fear and Control: Working with Young People Who Self-Harm*. Ross-on-Wye: PCCS Books.

Tucker, S. (2015) 'Still Not Good Enough! Must Try Harder: An Exploration of Social Defences in Schools.' In D. Armstrong and M. Rustin (eds) *Social Defences Against Anxiety: Explorations in a Paradigm*. London: Karnac Books.

Winnicott, D.W. (1958) *Through Paediatrics to Psychoanalysis: Collected Papers*. London: Karnac Books.

Winnicott, D.W. (1962) 'The Beginnings of a Formulation of an Appreciation and Criticism of Klein's Envy Statement.' In C. Winnicott, R. Shepherd and M. Davis (eds) *Psycho-Analytic Explorations: D.W. Winnicott*. (1989). London: Karnac Books.

Winnicott, D.W. (1963) 'The Development of the Capacity for Concern.' In *The Maturational Processes and the Facilitating Environment*. London: Hogarth Press.

Winnicott, D.W. (1965) *The Maturational Processes and the Facilitating Environment*. London: Hogarth Press.

Winnicott, D.W. (1967) 'The Concept of Clinical Regression Compared with That of Defence Organisation.' In C. Winnicott, R. Shepherd and M. Davis (eds) *Psycho-Analytic Explorations: D.W. Winnicott*. (1989) London: Karnac Books.

Winnicott, D.W. (1971) *Playing and Reality*. London: Routledge.

Winnicott, D.W. (1989a) 'Melanie Klein: On Her Concept of Envy.' In C. Winnicott, R. Shepherd and M. Davis (eds.) *Psycho-Analytic Explorations*. London: Karnac Books.

Winnicott, D.W. (1989b) 'The Use of an Object.' In C. Winnicott, R. Shepherd and M. Davis (eds) *Psycho-Analytic Explorations*. London: Karnac Books.

Yalom, I.D. (1970) *The Theory and Practice of Group Psychotherapy*. New York, NY: Basic Books.

Yalom, I.D. (1980) *Existential Psychotherapy*. New York, NY: Basic Books.

Index

abuse 63–4
adolescence 21, 29, 32–3, 56, 105–6, 139
advice 16, 22, 46, 49, 107, 122, 130
Alexander, L. 45, 106
Allison, E. 182
aloneness 29, 75, 161
Alvarez, A. 45, 138
ambivalence 69, 78, 148
    see also mixed feelings
anger 26–27, 29–30, 32–4, 36, 46, 60, 79, 82, 86, 89, 91–103, 127, 137–8, 142, 157–8, 161
    management 79, 91–2, 95–6
anxiety 32, 34–5, 39, 41, 43, 45–6, 49, 57–60, 77, 80, 87, 106, 108, 120, 122, 128, 136, 142, 167, 169, 172, 183
    collective 108
    disorders 49
    exam 167
    existential 175–6, 181
    institutional 51–6, 111
    paedophilic 141
Association For Young People's Health 106
asylum seekers 64
attachment 44, 72, 92, 107, 114, 182
attention-seeking 85–6
authority-figures 26, 116, 162
autobiographical story 44, 79–84, 87–8

Beckett, S. 172
betrayal 40, 92–3
Bion, W. 34, 54, 129
Bollas, C. 161
Bond, M. 31
borderline personality disorder 52
boundaries 10, 48–9, 71, 110–11, 113–19, 145
Bramley, W. 41, 126, 139
bullying 14, 46, 79, 88, 142

Casement, P. 35
Clarkson, P. 125
clinical judgment 41, 65, 123, 130–1
cognitive behaviour therapy 57
computer games 86, 138
confidentiality 13–14, 34, 47–8, 156
containment 33, 112, 122, 128–9, 181
core
    conflict 41
    complex 75
cutting 38, 53, 154–8
    see also self-harm

Davies, J. 107
death 34, 173–4, 176
    instinct 164
defences 15–16, 39, 41, 83–4, 87, 92, 96, 100, 102–3, 137, 147–9, 170–2
dependence 31–2, 69–72, 75–7
    see also independence
depression 41, 49, 106–7, 136, 142

CPI Antony Rowe
Eastbourne, UK
September 12, 2024